D0188300

STEAM'S LAST STAND

Mike Esau
STEAM'S LAST STAND

A 40th anniversary tribute to the end of British Railways steam

· RAILWAY HERITAGE ·
from
The NOSTALGIA *Collection*

© Mike Esau 2008

All rights reserved. No part of this publication may be reproduced, stored in a retrieval system or transmitted, in any form or by any means, electronic, mechanical, photocopying, recording or otherwise, without prior permission in writing from Silver Link Publishing Ltd.

First published in 2008

British Library Cataloguing in Publication Data

A catalogue record for this book is available from the British Library.

ISBN 978 1 85794 311 5

Silver Link Publishing Ltd
The Trundle
Ringstead Road
Great Addington
Kettering
Northants NN14 4BW

Tel/Fax: 01536 330588
email: sales@nostalgiacollection.com
Website: www.nostalgiacollection.com

Printed and bound in the Czech Republic

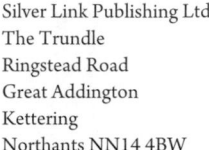

Half title **Lostock Hall shed: 'Britannia' 4-6-2 No 70013** *Oliver Cromwell*
Personifying 'Steam's Last Stand', and proudly displaying its '10A' Carnforth shedplate, No 70013 has been beautifully cleaned ready to work an 'end of steam' rail tour on 4 August 1968. By this time the shed foreman had given up trying to keep enthusiasts out of the shed, so there is something of an 'open house' at this Lancashire depot. On the left is an English Electric Type 4 diesel (later Class 40), which took over from the 'Britannias' many of the principal passenger workings on the West Coast Main Line.

Frontispiece **Near Burton & Holme: 8F 2-8-0**
On a still winter's day the impressive exhaust from the 8F is going so high that even the 6cm x 9cm format of my camera could not capture its full extent. The locomotive is heading north towards Oxenholme with a mixed freight.

Title page **Bolton shed: 5MT 4-6-0 No 45110**
Two footplatemen take a break at the shed not long before its closure – maybe they are discussing what changes the end of steam will produce. Bolton's No 45110 was destined to be a lucky locomotive as it was purchased for preservation in 1969 and can now be seen at the Severn Valley Railway.

Left **Warrington Bank Quay: 'Britannia' 4-6-2 No 70011, formerly** *Hotspur*
The fireman looks out of the cab of the 'Britannia', which has just been given the road to the south with a parcels train. This locomotive was one of the batch originally allocated to Norwich in May 1951 to work on Liverpool Street line expresses. It was transferred to the London Midland Region at the end of 1963, being withdrawn in December 1967. Sadly, in common with so many others of the class at the time, it looks rather run down, having lost its nameplates.

INTRODUCTION

I feel it was entirely appropriate that steam finished on the London Midland Region (LMR) in the North West, where the world's first commercially successful railway was opened between Liverpool to Manchester in 1830. Of all the BR Regions, the London Midland was surely the quintessential steam railway of the industrial age. Who could forget the sound of the exhaust from the big Stanier locomotives and their sonorous hooters, as they plunged into dank, sulphurous tunnels or climbed through the windswept fells?

When I first started this book my plan was to confine the pictures to the last two years or so of LMR steam working in the North West, which finished in August 1968. However, I soon realised that this would make for a rather depressing selection of photographs, dominated by shots of run-down Class 5s, 8Fs and Standard 9Fs. I therefore decided to expand my coverage to take in the last 11 years

from 1958 to 1968. Rather than arranging the photographs in sections or chapters as in my two previous 'Memories' books, I have set out the pictures to run through in a broadly chronological order to show the gradual run-down of steam, which culminated with the famous special 'farewell' trains on 4 and 11 August 1968.

By covering 11 years, I have been able to include main-line steam featuring the more interesting and glamorous locomotives such as BR 'Britannia' 'Pacifics', rebuilt 'Scots', 'Jubilees', 'Patriots', 'Princess Royals' and of course the superb 'Princess Coronations', a class that was for ever linked to the West Coast Main Line in the North West.

Sadly, all the 'namers' had been progressively withdrawn by the end of 1967 as the delivery of new Type 4 diesels gathered pace, save for 'Britannia' No 70013 *Oliver Cromwell* and Class 5 No 45156 *Ayrshire Yeomanry*, both of which worked trains on the last day of steam, 4 August 1968. The charismatic 'Princess Royals' and the unrebuilt 'Patriots' had all gone by the end of 1962, the 'Princess Coronations' by the end of 1964, the rebuilt 'Patriots' and 'Scots' by the end of 1965, the 'Clans' by the end of 1966, and the 'Jubilees' and all but the one 'Britannia' by the end of 1967. Of the more workaday and mundane locomotives, I was in time to see the last Lancashire &

Newton Heath shed: 5MT 4-6-0 No 45025
Like sister locomotive No 45110, No 45025 also survived into preservation and is now based at the Strathspey Railway at Aviemore. Built at the Vulcan Foundry in August 1934, it is the oldest of the preserved Class 5s. On 5 May 1968 it worked the last up Heysham to Manchester 'Belfast Boat Train', which is depicted on page 122.

Yorkshire Railway 2-4-2Ts and 0-6-0s at work, tough little machines that lasted almost as long as some of the more modern classes, such as the Stanier and Fairburn 2-6-4Ts.

Inevitably because of limitations of time and money it was not possible to visit everywhere in the North West, but I hope that the photographs in this book give a good representative picture of the last days of steam. Strangely, though, in all my travels I cannot recall coming across any other photographers out on the line, except of course towards the end when so many realised that time was running out. Incidentally, all my photographs are what I call 'organic', with no digitally originated additions, deletions or colours – what you see is as it was!

My own association with the North West goes back many years, although I was born in the South East of England and have lived there for most of my life. However, towards the end of the war I went to stay with my uncle's parents, Mr and Mrs Morgan, at Ringley, just south-east of Bolton. Mr Morgan was the headmaster of the local church school, which I attended for the comparatively short time I was living in Ringley. Their house was located on the eastern side of the valley, through which the then very polluted River Irwell flowed, and gave an uninterrupted view of the line from Bolton to Manchester. Kearsley was the local station, reached by a steep flight of steps from the A667 road. It was here that I first remember LMS steam, such as 2Ps on local trains to Manchester, and I enjoyed watching them emerge from Farnworth Tunnel before arriving at the station, their brakes squealing as they drew to a stop.

After coming out of the army following VJ Day, my uncle and his

Andrew Barclay 0-4-0ST No 1223 photographed at Greening's on 15 May 1959. *Jim Peden, Industrial Railway Society Collection*

wife eventually settled at Tarleton between Preston and Southport, not far from where the West Lancs Light Railway now operates. This was an ideal holiday base from which to undertake railway trips in the North West using Hesketh Bank station, or by catching a Ribble bus on the Southport to Preston service, which came through Tarleton village. Later on, as I relate in the caption to the picture on page 81, I was posted to RAF Weeton near Blackpool for technical training during my National Service. Providing you could get a lift down to Kirkham station, the camp was a good starting-off point for visits to the West Coast Main Line when time allowed.

Connections with the North West were destined to continue when I married in 1962, since my wife's family lived just to the south of Warrington. My father-in-law was the technical director at N. Greening & Son, wire weavers and perforated metal makers at Warrington, whose works was located adjacent to the West Coast Main Line. The firm had its own steam locomotive, Andrew Barclay 0-4-0ST No 1223 *Colin McAndrew*, so here was another railway connection! This locomotive went to the Chasewater Railway in 1966 where it is currently being restored to working order. Naturally I took advantage of our regular journeys to Warrington to photograph steam wherever I could as it was still very much in charge on the main line in the early 1960s. The lure of the north was very strong, so I often visited famous locations around Grayrigg, Shap and Ais Gill on the Settle & Carlisle (S&C) line.

At the end of 1958 there were something over 7,500 ex-LMS and BR Standard steam locomotives in service, though of course not all these operated in the North West. How the position had changed at the beginning of 1968, since by then the comparable figure was down to some 350 locomotives, comprising of a handful of classes.

Underlining that the end of steam was drawing near, the LMR's first purpose-built diesel maintenance depot was opened at Crewe in 1958. At the same time Crewe Works was completing construction of its last order for 30 9Fs. Of these, No 92250 was the final steam locomotive built at the works. It left on 15 December 1958 after a special ceremony to mark the event, but was destined to have only a short working life, being withdrawn in 1965, a mere seven years later.

Before the era of mass withdrawals, locomotives were generally cut up at the main works such as Crewe or Derby in the case of the LMR. However, because of orders for new diesel locomotives and routine overhauls, cutting-up work was passed to private contractors such as the now famous Woodham Brothers at Barry. Large dumps of withdrawn locomotives formed, the one at Heapey illustrated on page 15 being an early example. Other dumps that appeared on the LMR were at Badnall Wharf, north of Norton Bridge, and Winsford, which in March 1959 together contained a total of some 50 locomotives awaiting disposal.

As steam was progressively replaced by diesel locomotives on the LMR, many of the sheds that had been visited by generations of enthusiasts in steam days closed. One of the most famous, Crewe North (5A), for so many years the home of a number of Stanier 'Pacifics', closed to steam in May 1965. Other depots, affected by regional boundary changes, lost their memorable shed codes, such as Carlisle (Upperby), which from January 1958 became 12B instead of 12A. Carlisle (Kingmoor), previously a 'Sassenach' under the mantle of the Scottish Region as 68A, became 12A. In later years there were more changes – for example, the once important shed at Newton Heath, 26A, became the rather mundane-sounding 9D, though Carnforth retained its 'A-list' status as 10A, operating in the front line right to the end of steam, as the picture on page 122 shows. Suffix letters in shed codes that were previously unknown appeared; for instance, where would you have found an 'M' shed in the 1950s, yet Southport, the once familiar 27C, became the almost anonymous 8M.

While towards the end the majority of sheds contained sad lines of withdrawn or stored locomotives, some, like Bolton, still made an attempt to keep up the old standards. The photograph on page 113 shows some of the allocation of its Stanier Class 5s and 8Fs, smartly turned out and lined up in front of the shed. As depots closed there were ever fewer to visit, so comprehensive itineraries such as those set out in Aiden Fuller's *British Locomotive Shed Directory*, perhaps around the smoky suburbs of cities like Manchester, could no longer be enjoyed. Who can forget those memorable instructions in the *Directory*? For example, to reach Agecroft:

'...Board a Salford Corporation No 81 (Irlams O' Th' Height) bus in Bridge Street off Deansgate, and alight at Bank Lane. Walk to the end of this road, passing under Irlams O' Th' Height station, and a footpath leads from the right-hand side across a field to the shed. Journey time 25 minutes.'

What memories of the 1950s these words evoke!

So arrived the fateful day of 4 August 1968 when, with many others, I photographed the beautifully cleaned *Oliver Cromwell* standing proudly outside the shed at Lostock Hall, a location that would ever more be linked with the end of steam. In those days Lostock Hall itself was just a modest village on the southern outskirts of Preston. The 3rd of August had seen the very last ordinary passenger train using steam haulage, the 9.25pm train from Preston to Liverpool Exchange hauled by Class 5 No 45318. *The Railway Observer* reported that, in charge of driver E. Heyes from Lostock Hall, the train reached a top speed of 78mph through Maghull, a fitting end to an era. On 4 August, never had so many steam enthusiast specials operated during a single day. British Railways also ran its own train from Manchester to Southport in the afternoon hauled by Class 5 No 45110. In the gathering gloom at Hoghton I photographed my last British Railways steam train, the very-late-running Railway Correspondence & Travel Society special, which is shown on page 126. Finally, on 11 August came British Railways' famous, or perhaps infamous, '15 Guinea Special' illustrated in colour on page VIII. Although at the time it seemed to present a last chance to see steam on the main line, for me the magic had gone since the real farewell had been the weekend before.

As with my two 'Memories' books published by Silver Link, I would like to thank once again the 'two Johns', John Edgington and John Gilks, who looked through the photographs and fully answered my queries. David, my brother, with whom I shared some trips to the North West, has also helped. My recollection of some of the places I visited on these trips 40 or more years ago has not been perfect, so John Webster has been of immense help with his detailed knowledge of the railways of the North West. I am also greatly indebted to Roger Cruse for not only lending me his copies of *The Railway Observer* for the years 1958 to 1968, but also for allowing me to use his excellent colour photograph of the '15 Guinea Special' crossing Ais Gill Viaduct, which appears on page VIII. Callum McLeod, the Managing Editor of *The Railway Observer*, generously consented to me using extracts from the journal in this book. The detail contained in *The Railway Observer* is quite amazing and we owe a great debt of gratitude to those members of the Railway Correspondence & Travel Society who meticulously recorded all that information so many years ago. Bob Darvill of the Industrial Railway Society came up trumps with information about the locomotives used at Greening's works in Warrington. My thanks, of course, as always for the support given to me by Peter Townsend, Will Adams and the team at Silver Link Publishing and for making this book possible. As with previous books, my wife Alison has not only helped enormously with the arrangement of the photographs, but has also made many constructive comments and suggestions. She has also been an invaluable 'second pair of eyes' with the proof-reading.

Mike Esau
Richmond, Surrey
2008

Preston: 2P 4-4-0 No 40681

This is a typical Lancashire scene on the London Midland Region in the late 1950s. Wigan (L&Y) shed's 4-4-0 is waiting to leave for Southport with a local train. There is much to be seen and enjoyed in this photograph, such as the overall roof of the station, the decorative water column and the two station staff chatting before the train leaves. No 40681 was one of the last 2Ps to be withdrawn, surviving until August 1962.

Above Hawes: 4MT 2-6-4T No 42278, 23 January 1958

Some lines in the North West closed to passengers before the 1963 Beeching Report. One such was the Garsdale to Hawes branch, which saw the end of passenger services on 14 March 1959. Here is the 4.25pm train ready to depart for Hellifield. On the last day Stanier 2-6-4T No 42492 officiated. *The Railway Observer* records that the three-coach train conveyed 53 passengers from Garsdale to Hawes and an even larger contingent on the final departure. Two motor coaches had to be hired to bring the residents of Hawes back home from remote Garsdale station!

Right **Torver: 2MT 2-6-2T No 41221**

A few months earlier than Hawes, the line from Foxfield to Coniston closed on 6 October 1958. On weekdays only, eight trains made the 25-minute journey of almost 10 miles along the branch. Note the steps on the right used for gaining access to the station lights.

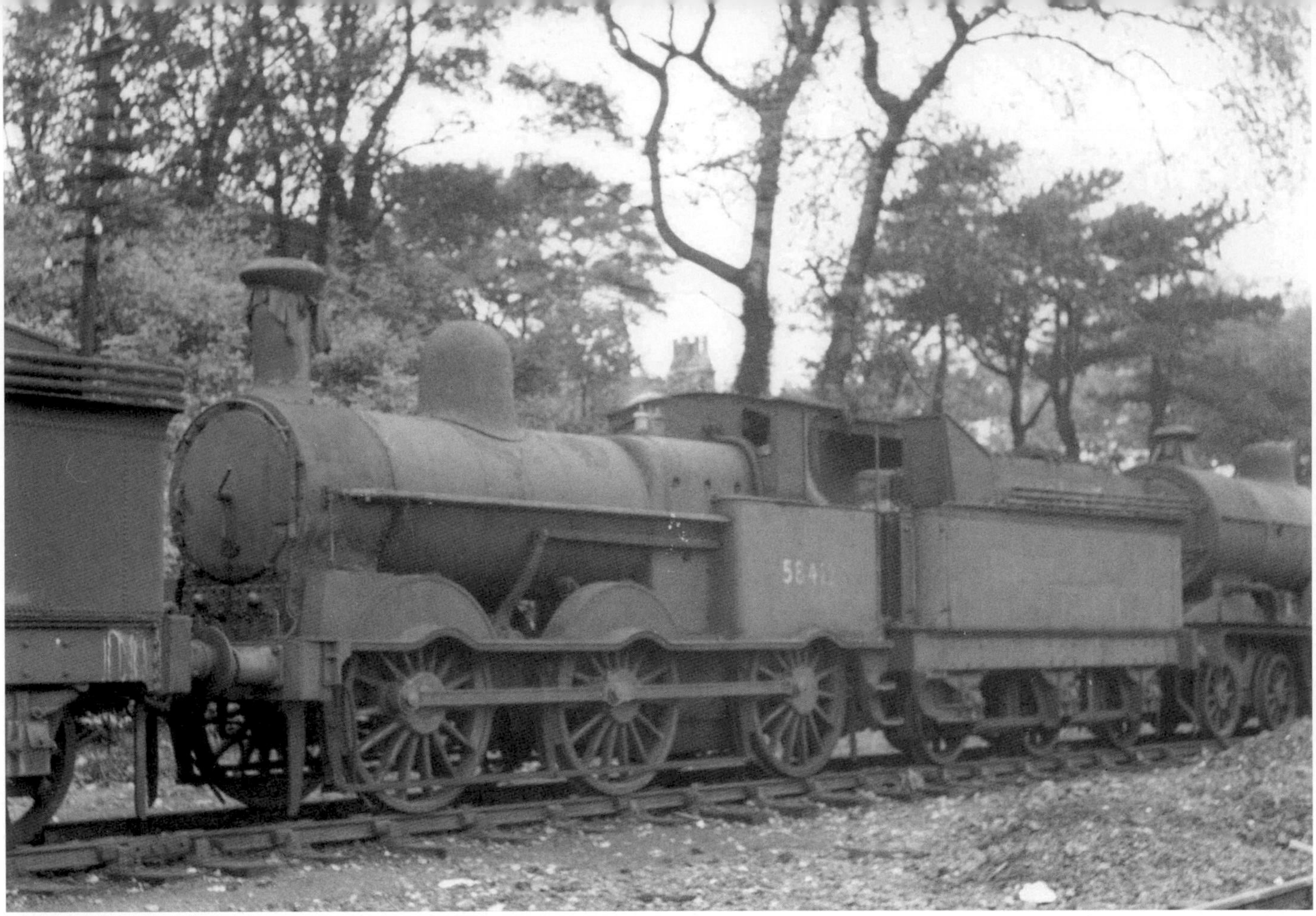
58412

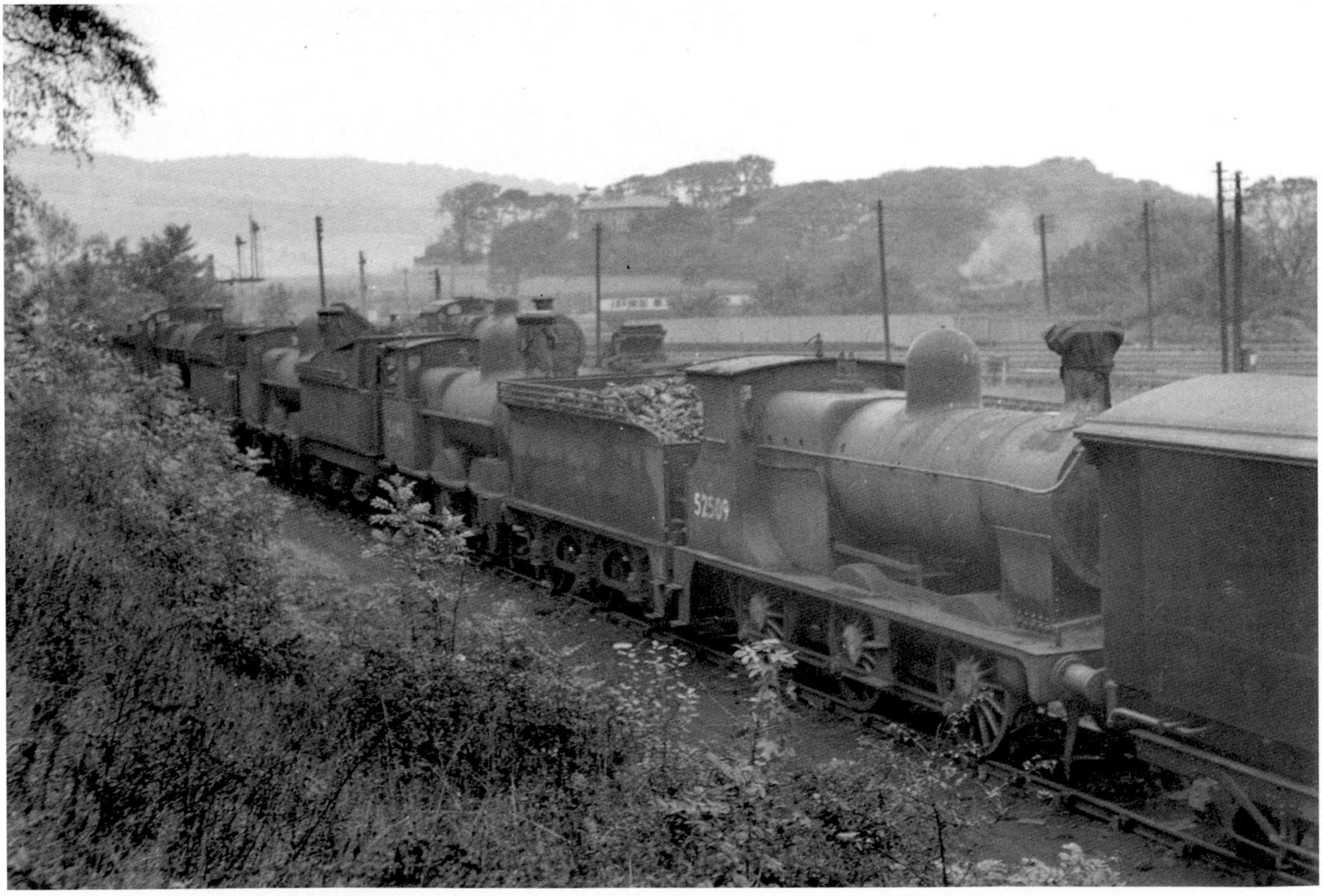
52509

Left **Carnforth shed: 2F 0-6-0 No 58412**
No 58412 was one of the last three LNWR 'Cauliflower' 0-6-0s to remain in service. Like a survivor from another age, the locomotive is in store at the shed in 1955. It was withdrawn at the end of the year, and later on it would be the turn of more recent Midland Railway, Lancashire & Yorkshire Railway and LMS designs to disappear. Long lines of withdrawn locomotives became a common sight at sheds throughout the North West of England as the end of steam approached.

Below left **Carnforth shed: 3F 0-6-0 No 52509**
Also in the line of relics stored at Carnforth was this Furness Railway locomotive, of which only six came into British Railways stock, this one being withdrawn at the end of 1956. The rough sacking over the chimney was generally a sure sign that the locomotive's days were numbered. The last survivor of the class, No 52510, lasted until August 1957.

Above right **Rose Grove shed: 2P 2-4-2T No 50655**
The attractive Lancashire & Yorkshire Railway 2-4-2Ts enlivened the scene in the North West as late as 1961, notably No 50850 of Southport, which appears on page 26. However, this example, stored at the end of a siding by the side of the shed, looks unlikely to steam again and was withdrawn in June 1956.

Below **Bolton shed: 3F 0-6-0 No 52443**
By 1959, when this photograph was taken, the majority of these long-lived L&Y locomotives had been withdrawn, but Horwich Works was still dealing with the occasional one. It is the end of the road though for No 52443, which, after a hard working life of 59 years, was withdrawn in November 1959. The locomotive's worksplate on the splasher over the centre wheel has already been removed. Also seen on the scrap road are a Fowler 0-8-0 and a 'Jinty' 0-6-0T.

Above Lostock Hall shed: 4MT 2-6-4T No 42481 and 3F 0-6-0 No 52523
The old order at Lostock Hall is represented by the Stanier tank and the L&Y 0-6-0 standing outside the soot-encrusted shed on this gloomy day. Such was the usefulness of the 0-6-0 that it lasted until September 1962, before its duties were taken over by 350hp diesel shunters. The more modern 2-6-4T did little better than the old 0-6-0, being withdrawn in September 1964.

Below Lostock Hall: 3F 0-6-0 No 52429
Typical of what was for many years a commonplace sight in goods yards all over the North West is this L&Y 0-6-0 pausing between shunting duties. The weather must have been wet earlier in the day, because the sheet giving the enginemen in the exposed cab some protection from the rain has been taken down and is draped over the side of the cab. No 52429 was withdrawn in October 1960.

Bolton Trinity Street: 3F 0-6-0 No 52393 and 5MT 4-6-0 45220
In the foreground of this 1959 picture a Class 5 is arriving on a train from Manchester, while the Bolton-shedded L&Y 0-6-0 waits in the up platform to allow one of the smart, newly introduced diesel multiple units to leave the bay platform bound for Rochdale. Judging by the number of four-wheel vans parked outside it and the merchandise on the trailers in the yard, the massive goods warehouse seems to be very busy.

Bolton Trinity Street: 3F 0-6-0 No 52523
Here is No 52523 again, this time trundling into Bolton station across the Blackburn lines with a short goods train from the Chorley direction. The locomotive looks a little tired but may have been into Horwich Works since I last saw it (page 12). The long footbridge across the station at this point was an excellent vantage point for spotters, some of whom can be seen through the latticework.

Above Heapey: Summer 1959

Hidden away on the line between Blackburn and Chorley was Heapey, site of a secure storage depot for Royal Ordnance Factory (ROF), Chorley. In the late 1950s and early 1960s the depot was used as the resting place for withdrawn locomotives mostly destined for cutting up at Horwich Works. Up to 16 locomotives were present in 1959 and among those seen here are 3F 0-6-0 No 43890, 3F 0-6-0 No 52237, 2F 0-6-0ST No 51404 and 2P 2-4-2T No 50647.

Below Bolton shed: 1959

As the pace of withdrawals increased so did the lines of locomotives awaiting cutting up, which is the fate of this forlorn group at Bolton. From left to right are 4F 0-6-0 No 44000, Fowler 7F 0-8-0 No 49662, 3F 0-6-0T No 47440, another Fowler 7F 0-8-0, and an L&Y 3F 0-6 0. All the rather ponderous Fowler 7Fs (nicknamed 'Austin Sevens') had gone by the beginning of 1962.

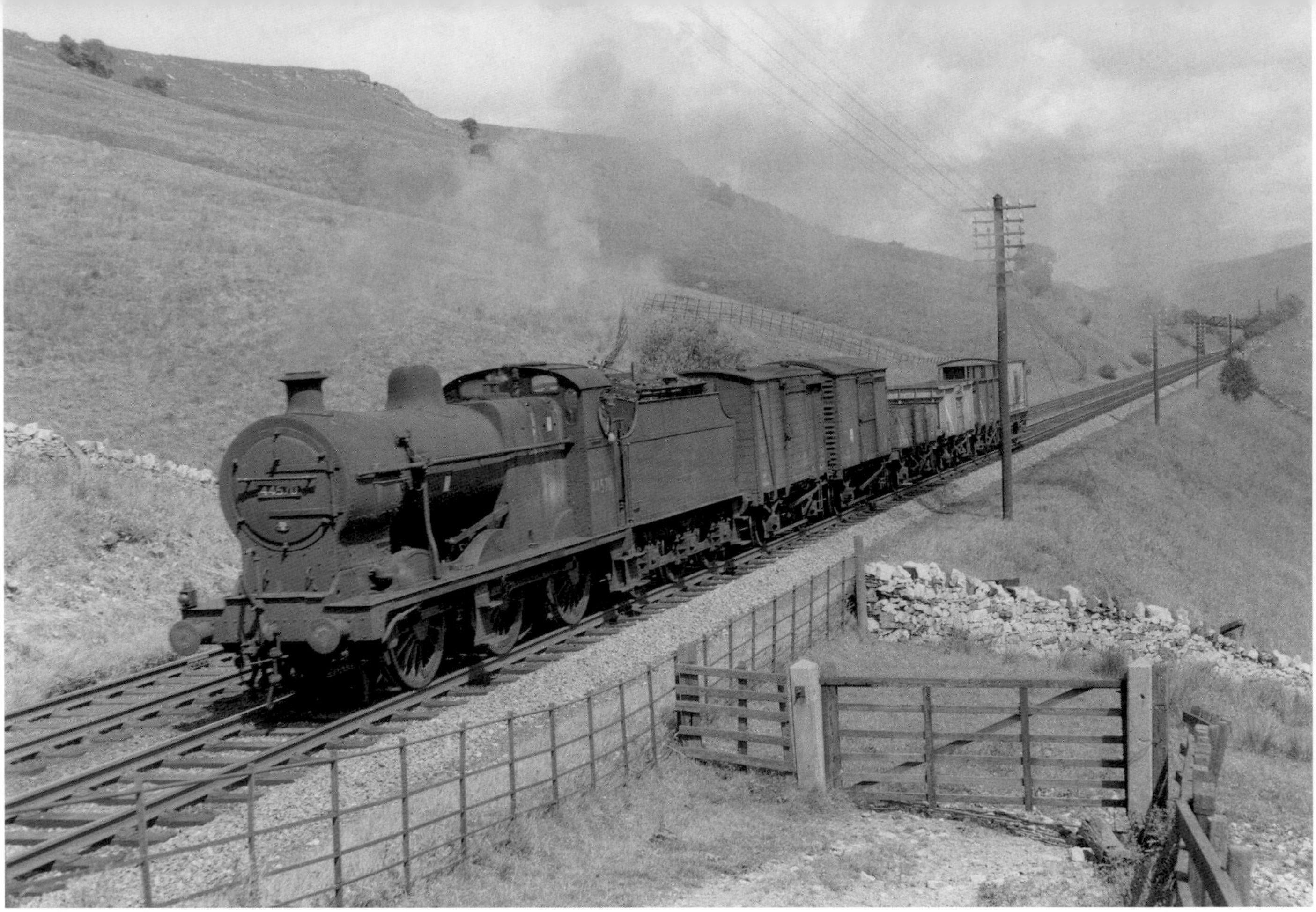

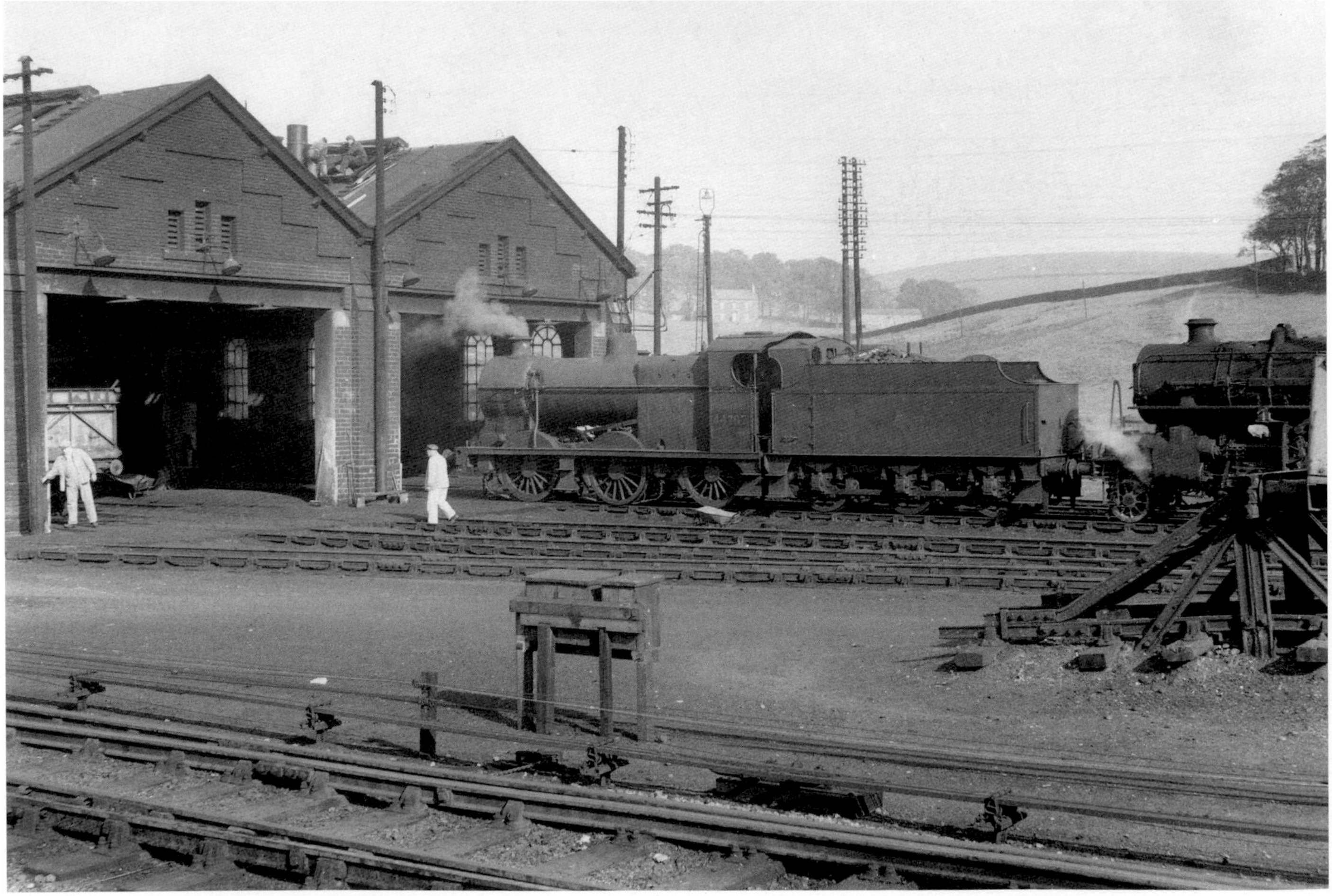

Left **Mallerstang Common: 4F 0-6-0 No 44570**
The 4Fs were long associated with the Settle & Carlisle (S&C) line, and as late as 1962 they were still working slower freights. This up working in August 1961 is on the 1 in 100 climb to Ais Gill summit. The final two 4Fs, Nos 44377 and 44525, withdrawn in October 1966, were employed as shunters at Crewe Works, their final main-line duties being on the stores train at the end of August 1966.

Below left **Hellifield shed: 4F 0-6-0 No 44282, 1959**
The 4F standing outside the shed is fitted with a tender cab to give the crew some protection against the wild weather common over the S&C, especially when working tender-first or on snow-clearing duties. Behind the 4F is an Ivatt 2-6-0. Hellifield shed (24H) was closed on 17 June 1963, marking the decline in the status of this once important centre, the southern gateway of the line northward over the fells to Carlisle.

Above right **Hellifield shed: 2P 4-4-0 No 40685**
Adjacent to the turntable, Hellifield's 2P is on stand-by duty, ready to pilot the locomotive of any northbound passenger train that might require assistance on the long climb to Ais Gill summit. No 40685 was something of a special 2P since it was probably one of the last of its class employed on main-line piloting duties in the North West. It was withdrawn in July 1961.

Below **Ribblehead Viaduct: 2P 4-4-0 and 5MT 4-6-0, Summer 1959**
Maybe it is No 40685 that is assisting the Class 5 on the northbound 'Thames-Clyde Express' at Ribblehead, which includes an ex-LMS restaurant car in its formation. The scaffolding on one of the arches shows that repair work is being carried out on the viaduct. In some 3 miles the train will reach Blea Moor Tunnel where the worst of the climb will be over.

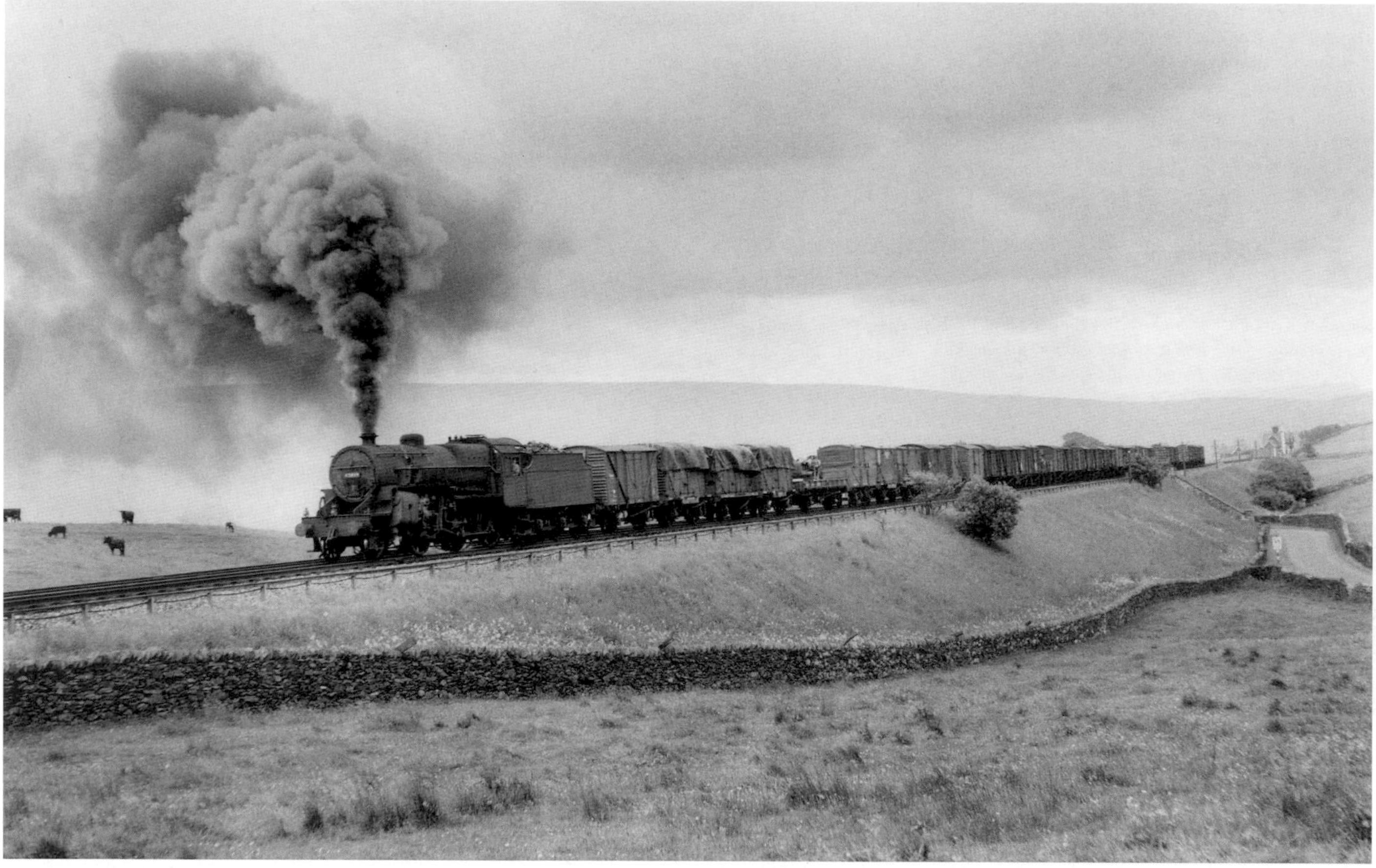

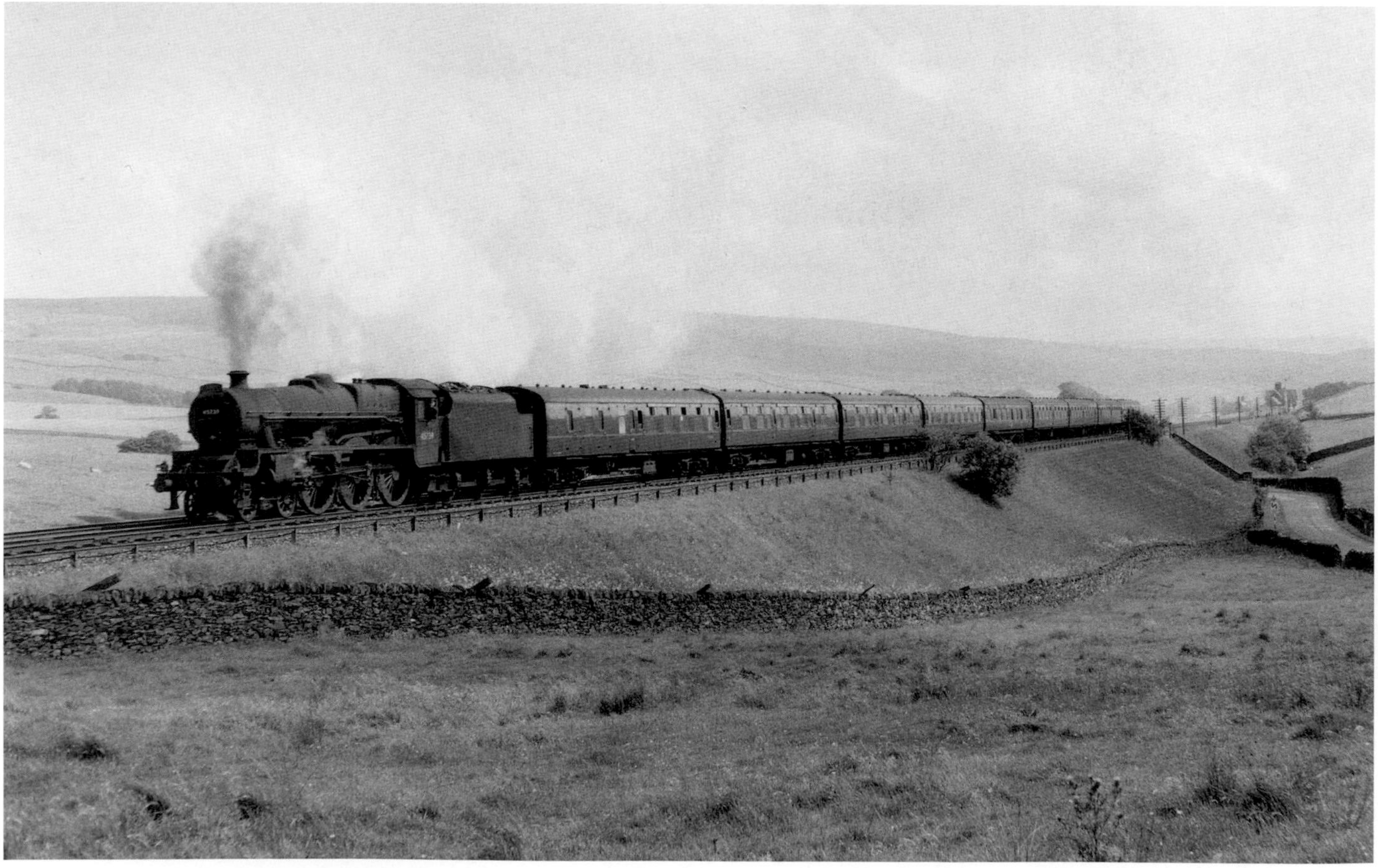

Opposite **Near Horton-in-Ribblesdale: 5MT 2-6-0 No 42899 and 'Jubilee' 4-6-0 No 45739 *Ulster*, 1960**

The Hughes-designed 'Crab' 2-6-0s were regular performers on freight workings over the S&C, but this one is having a bit of a struggle up the 1 in 100 gradient with its long northbound fully-fitted freight. On the right of the picture is the B6479 road, which followed the line for some distance, providing ready access to good photographic locations. No 42899 was one of the earlier members of the class to be withdrawn in December 1962, but a handful soldiered on to the end of 1966.

Regular motive power for the principal express passenger trains was the 'Jubilee' Class, one of which is working the northbound 'Waverley' express from St Pancras to Edinburgh Waverley. It was due off Hellifield at 2.44pm, arriving in the Scottish city just before 7.00pm. No 45739 was one of the last 'Jubilees' to be built and was withdrawn in January 1967. By this time the few 'Jubilees' still working on the S&C, such as Nos 45562 *Alberta* and 45593 *Kolhapur*, had attracted a large enthusiast following who travelled behind them whenever possible.

South of Ribblehead: A3 4-6-2 No 60077 *The White Knight*, 1960
In the spring of 1960 the first A3s arrived at Holbeck shed, Leeds, from Neville Hill, and were to be followed by a few more from the Newcastle area, made redundant by Type 4 diesels. They were used by Holbeck on principal trains over the S&C with some success, such as the up 'Thames-Clyde Express', seen in this picture. No 60077 was withdrawn in July 1964 from St Margaret's (Edinburgh) shed.

***Above* Hardrigg: 'Jubilee' 4-6-0 No 45721 *Impregnable*
Below Docker Hall: 'Jubilee' 4-6-0 No 45684 *Jutland* and rebuilt 'Royal Scot' 4-6-0**
Here are two West Coast steam-hauled main-line expresses of the early 1960s on Grayrigg bank before the Type 4 diesels began to take over the workings. Without the benefit of a banker from Oxenholme, No 45721 is having to work hard up the 1 in 106 gradient with its heavy train, which looks to be about 11 coaches with luggage vans front and rear.

Even on the West Coast Main Line, trains with 6P and 7P locomotives working in tandem were quite unusual, like this one photographed further down the bank. If the little horse-box behind the 'Scot' was in use, the horse might perhaps have been alarmed by the roar from the two big locomotives as they forged north!

Low Gill: 5MT 4-6-0 No 44886 and 4MT 2-6-4T

Before the advent of the M6 motorway Low Gill was a tranquil location set among the fells, which offered northbound trains a breather between the steep gradients of Grayrigg and Shap banks. Fitted with a snow plough beneath the buffer beam, the Class 5 is heading south with a lengthy partially fitted freight. To the right of the picture are railway cottages adjacent to the line to Clapham; this was sometimes used as a diversionary route for trains from the S&C, especially during the hard winter weather at the beginning of 1963. The Clapham to Low Gill line was taken up in June 1967.

Against the majestic background of the fells behind Howgill, the Fowler 2-6-4T is in charge of an up local train in August 1961.

Shap bank: Fowler 4MT 2-6-4T and Stanier/Fairburn 4MT 2-6-4T
These pictures show the two principal 2-6-4T types used to bank trains up Shap for many years. In the top picture a Fowler tank has just started away from Tebay, which can seen against the hillside in the background. Further up the bank near Scout Green the sheep seem unconcerned by the noise of the Fairburn tank as it assists a mixed freight hauled by a Class 5.

Shap Wells: Unrebuilt 'Patriot' 4-6-0 No 45505 *The Royal Army Ordnance Corps* **and 4MT 2-6-4T No 42098 with a 5MT 4-6-0**
Though there are signs of scorching on its smokebox door, No 45505, which is fitted with an earlier Stanier design of tender, seems to be having no difficulty climbing the 1 in 75 gradient with its fitted freight. No 45505 was withdrawn in June 1962 and all the unrebuilt locomotives had gone by the end of that year.

The 2-6-4Ts based at Tebay usually banked trains rather than being attached as a pilot locomotive, so maybe No 42098 has come on to this 13-coach train at Oxenholme. These Fairburn tanks took over from the Fowler tanks and by July 1964 there was only one of the latter left at Tebay. The Fairburns were in turn ousted by Standard Class 4 4-6-0s, and these were replaced by Clayton diesels from 1 January 1968, thus marking the end of steam banking over this famous stretch of line.

Above* Euxton Coal Sidings: 'Jubilee' 4-6-0 No 45582 *Central Provinces
Below* Preston: 'Jubilee' 4-6-0 No 45629 *Straits Settlements

The 'Jubilee' Class consisted of almost 200 locomotives, and their numbers meant that they played a prominent part in express passenger train workings in the North West before being ousted by the English Electric Type 4 diesels, 42 of which were destined for the London Midland Region in the 1960 main-line diesel programme. No 45582 is heading south on a train for Crewe and Euston and will shortly pass Euxton Junction, where the line to Chorley and Manchester diverged.

At Preston the morning light is catching the side of the locomotive as it prepares to leave with a train for the south.

Above **Long Barn, Hoghton: 'Jubilee' 4-6-0
No 45720 *Indomitable***
Right **Near Leyland: 'Jubilee' 4-6-0 No 45688
*Polyphemus***

Some of the 'Jubilees', like No 45720 seen here, were fitted with Fowler tenders, which looked a little puny for the locomotive, but they did have a certain visual appeal. On what is probably a return special from Blackpool to West Yorkshire, the rather careworn-looking *Indomitable* is climbing the 1 in 101 gradient near Hoghton with a train composed of ex-LMS stock. The locomotive was withdrawn in December 1962 at the end of a year when big inroads were made into the surviving members of the class.

On the main line near Leyland, south of Preston, No 45688 is heading south with a train for Euston. Note the tall signals with their co-acting arms and the ladder-stile on the right leading to the boarded crossing across the four-track main line – this would surely not be allowed in today's health-and-safety-conscious age.

LONDON STREET
EXCURSION PLATFORMS
78060
42293

50850
50850

Left **Southport: 2MT 2-6-0 No 78060 and 4MT 2-6-4T No 42293**

I have been lucky enough to capture a simultaneous departure from Chapel Street station – the train on the left is for the Wigan line and that on the right for Preston. The Standard 2-6-0 was destined to have a very short life, being built in October 1956 and withdrawn only 10 years later from Shrewsbury shed. Reflecting Southport's popularity as a seaside resort, the London Street Excursion Platforms can be seen on the right of the picture.

Below left **Southport: 2P 2-4-2T No 50850**

Southport shed was the home of the last two working L&Y 2-4-2Ts, Nos 50746 and 50850, which were employed on station pilot and shunting duties. The former was in poor condition and was withdrawn in February 1961; however, No 50850 kept going a little longer until withdrawal in October after two Ivatt 2-6-2Ts took over its duties. Here the 2-4-2T is hard at work shunting empty stock at this busy station. The line with the third rail is for the electric trains to Crossens.

Above right **Brock troughs: 5MT 4-6-0 No 44743**

Southport was also the home of the last surviving Caprotti Class 5; built in 1948, it was withdrawn in January 1966. As this picture shows, the Caprotti valve gear did nothing for the looks of the otherwise well-proportioned locomotive, which is heading south over the troughs with what is probably a summer Saturday extra.

Below **Hundred End: 4MT 2-6-4T No 42461**

The line from Southport to Preston closed to passengers on 6 September 1964. The station was set amidst rich agricultural land mainly given over to market gardening, its name deriving from the meeting of two 'hundreds', an ancient divisional name given to a portion of a county for administration or military purposes. The six-coach train, formed of ex-LMS main-line stock, is bound for Preston.

Approaching Warrington: 5MT 4-6-0

On the approach to Warrington from the north, the West Coast Main Line ran through surroundings that typified the atmosphere of the Lancashire industrial belt. The smoke from the Crosfield Soap Works, seen in the background, adds to the gloom and murk of this winter day as the sun tries to break through.

Above Weaver Navigation: 8F 2-8-0

The line between Warrington and Chester crossed the River Weaver and the Weaver Navigation waterway near Frodsham, providing a good location for photography. On a still winter's day the 8F crosses the Navigation with a westbound freight. The interesting line of vehicles on the right is waiting to join the A56 road.

Below Sutton Tunnel: 5MT 4-6-0

The Class 5 is about to enter the 1 mile 125 yards of Sutton Tunnel, situated a short distance west of the now closed Norton station. On the approach to the tunnel the line passes through an impressive cutting in the red sandstone.

Chester General: 5MT 4-6-0 No 45345 and rebuilt 'Royal Scot' 4-6-0 No 46150 *The Life Guardsman*, and 5MT 4-6-0 No 45044
Although only on the periphery of the 'North West', Chester was an interesting railway centre, so I have included some pictures taken there. Holyhead shed's No 46150 is ready to leave for the North Wales line, whilst the Class 5 waits on the through road; the 'Scot' was withdrawn from Carlisle (Upperby) in November 1963.

At the other end of the station, Chester's Class 5 No 45044 makes a smoky departure with a train for Crewe. The LNWR signals seen above the train are in marked contrast to the then modern Chester No 1 signal box on the right.

Chester General: 5MT 4-6-0s Nos 44951 and 44838, and 5MT 4-6-0 No 44807
No 44838 waits in the platform with a local train for the Shrewsbury line while No 44951, from 56D Mirfield shed, slowly comes through the station with an excursion train. The locomotive looks as if it has recently had a general overhaul, probably in Crewe Works. Meanwhile, No 44807 is passing the tall LNWR signal box with a train for Warrington and Manchester.

Left **Halton (Cheshire): 9F 2-10-0**
This picture speaks for itself, conveying the atmosphere of a late afternoon in winter as the sun sinks into the mist. The 9F is heading west past the station, which was closed in 1952. In the distance, another freight has been put into the loop.

Above **Warrington Dallam: 5MT 4-6-0s**
A weak sun on this cold winter morning in 1966 lights up a southbound freight train passing Dallam shed (8B). On 10 September 1962 the small shed at Warrington Arpley had closed and its allocation transferred to Dallam. In turn Dallam closed on 2 October 1967, and by November there were no steam sheds south of Preston on the West Coast Main Line.

Right **Norton: 'Jubilee' 4-6-0 No 45654 *Hood***
Most of the 'Jubilees' had been scrapped by the end of 1965, and *Hood* was one of the last of its class at work in the Warrington area, though in very poor condition; it was withdrawn in June 1966 from Newton Heath (9D). The locomotive's glory days are well over as it hauls this coal train approaching Norton station. A reminder of the markings that some of the unfortunate inhabitants of wartime ghettos were forced to carry, the locomotive is disfigured by a yellow diagonal stripe across the side of its cab denoting that it was prohibited from working south of Crewe after 1 September 1964, due to the commissioning of the electrification of the line.

Above and left **Blackrod: 4MT 2-6-4T No 42559 and 'Britannia' 4-6-2**

Blackrod was the junction for a branch of a mile or so to Horwich, where the ex-L&Y Works was located. For the benefit of the employees at the Works some services ran from and to Manchester Victoria in the morning and evening, but other trains just made the 4-minute journey along the branch. No 42559 is leaving the station with a stopping train for Manchester in 1959.

Later, in 1967, an unidentified 'Britannia' sweeps through with a Glasgow to Manchester express.

Above right and right **Blackrod: 8F 2-8-0 No 48111 and 2MT 2-6-2T No 84013**

On this crisp winter morning the 8F is accelerating through the station, with its attractive but soot-blackened chimneys.

At the other side of the station No 84013 is starting out with its push-and-pull train, which it is propelling on the short run to Horwich. Horwich Works ceased locomotive repairs on 6 May 1964, the last locomotive to be dealt with being 8F No 48756.

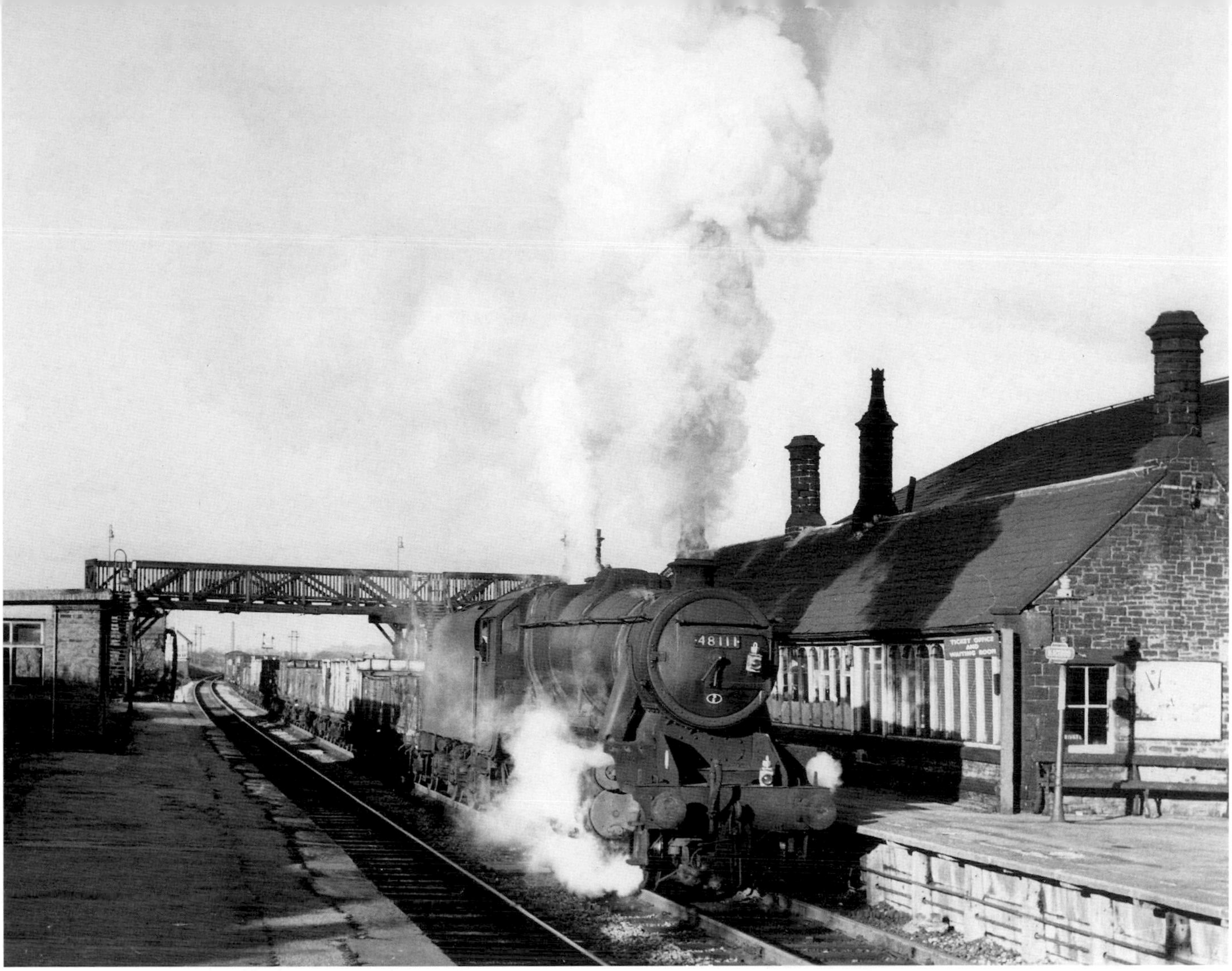
48111
TICKET OFFICE AND WAITING ROOM

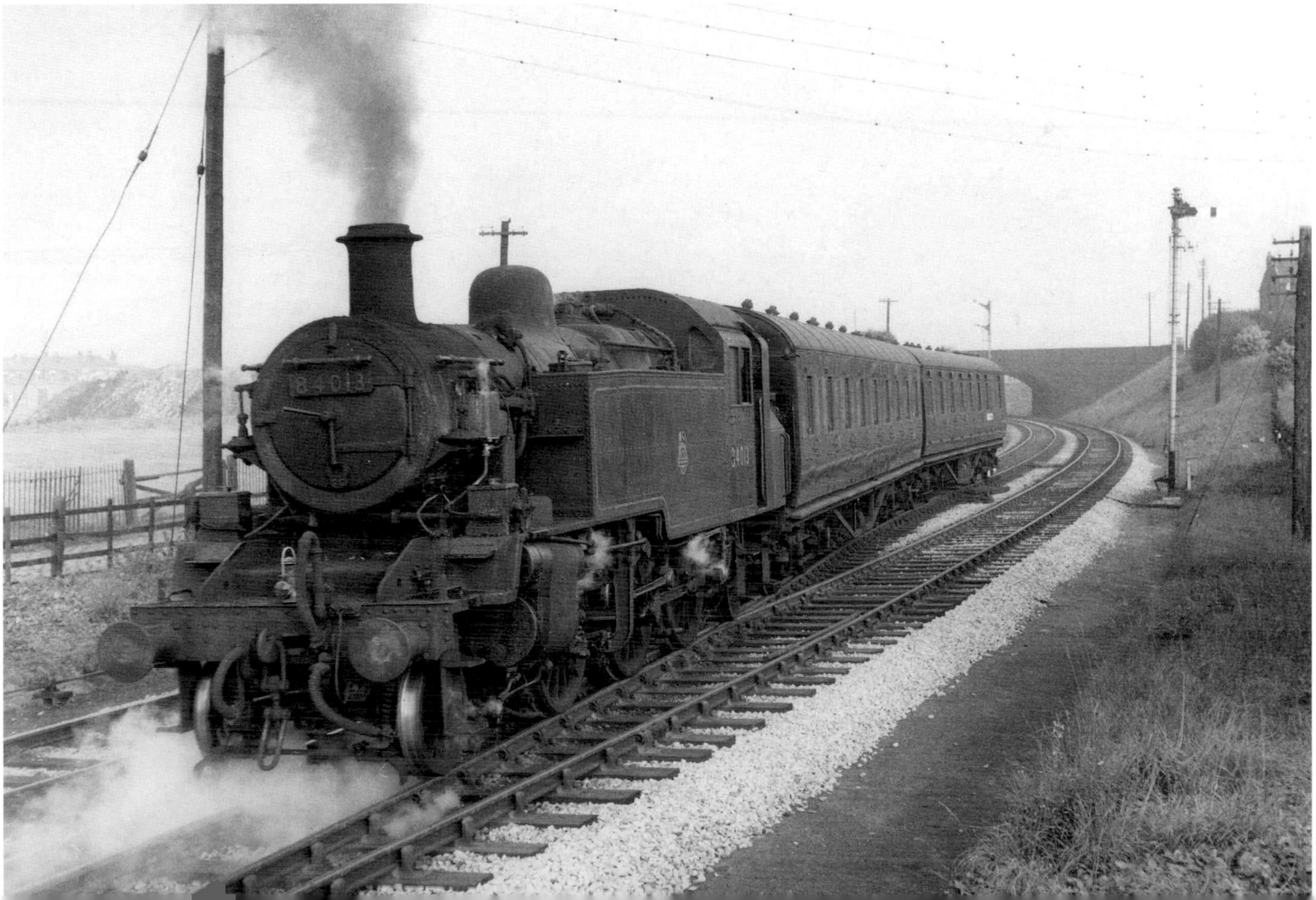
84013

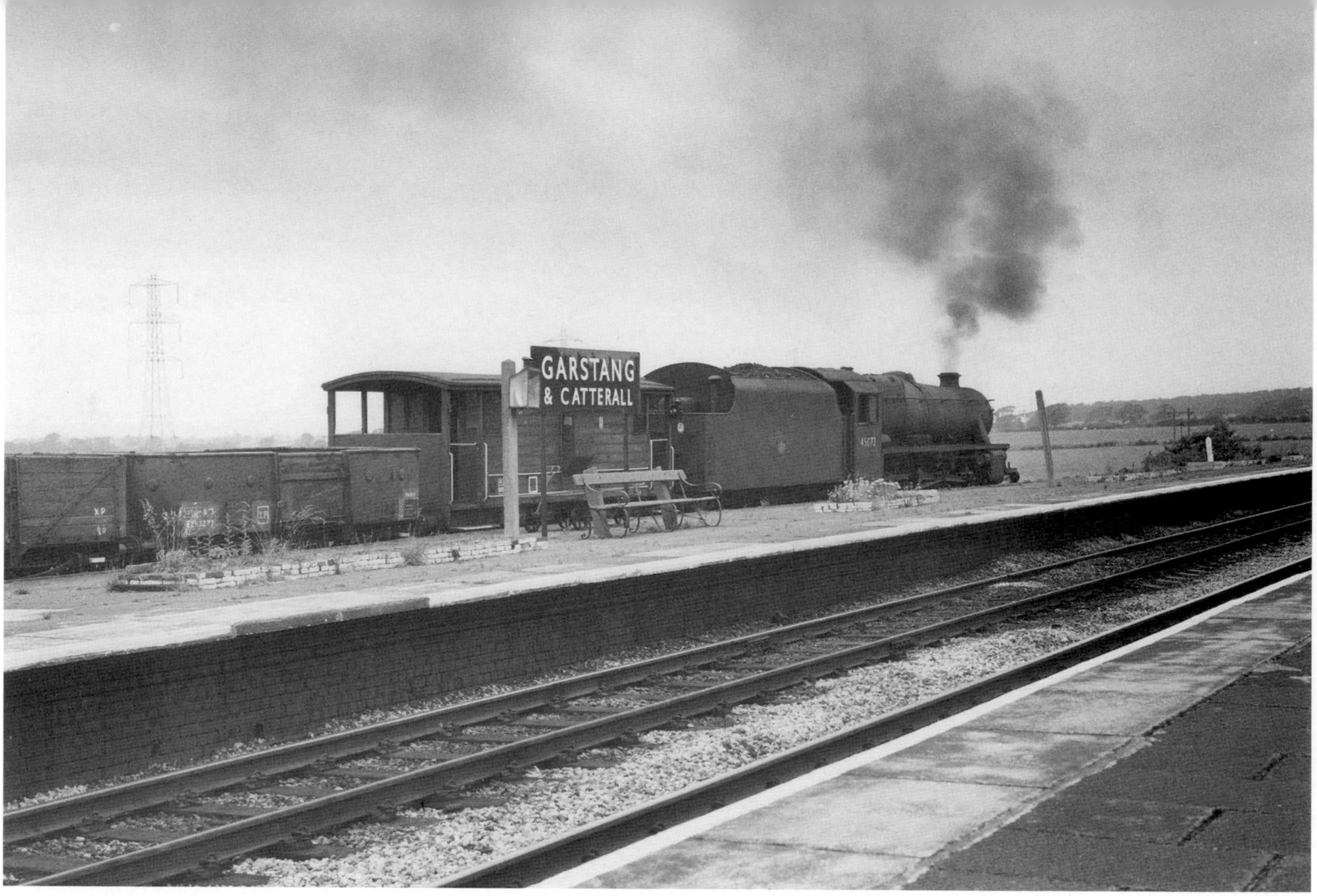
GARSTANG
& CATTERALL

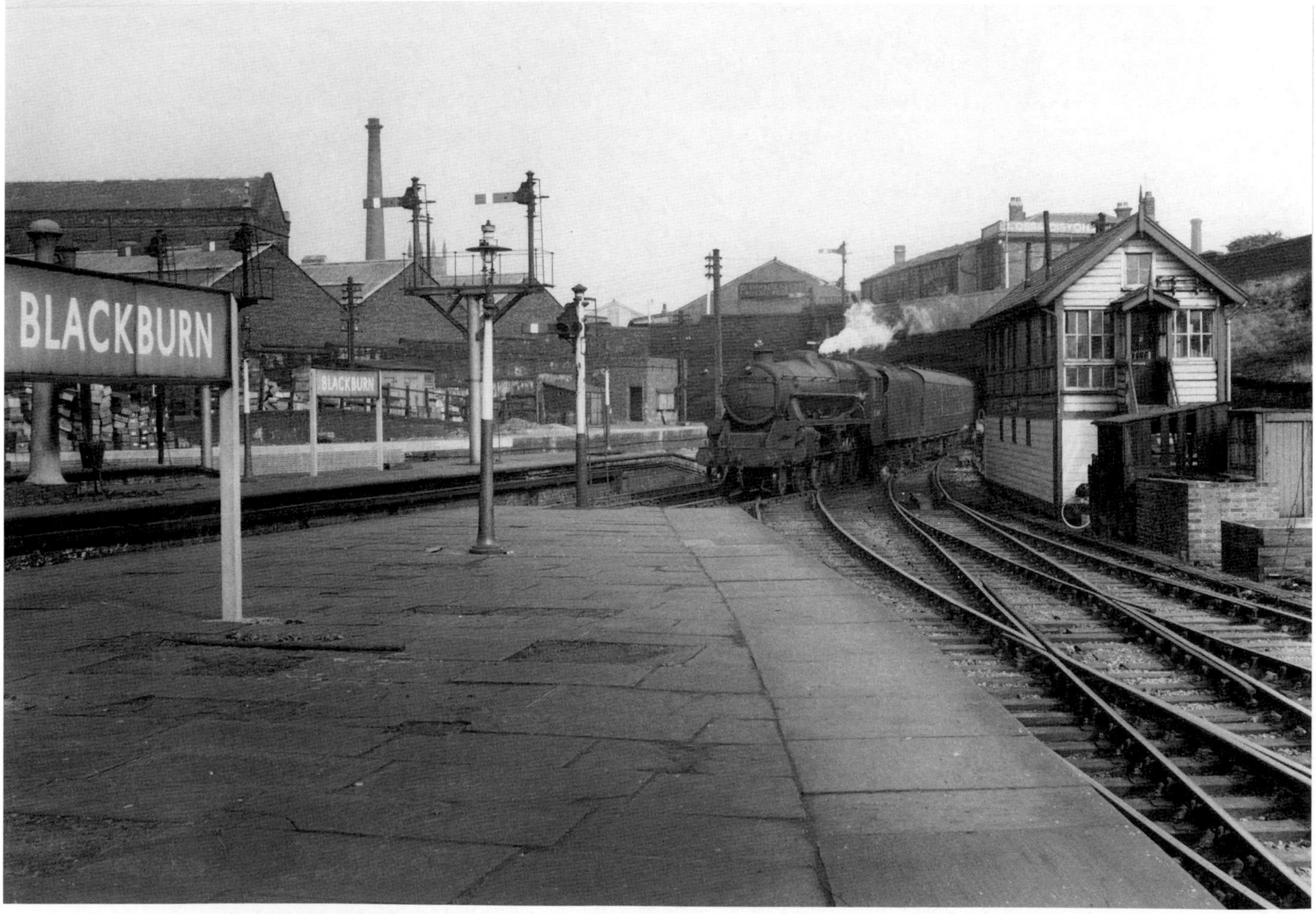
BLACKBURN
BLACKBURN

Left **Garstang & Catterall: 5MT 4-6-0 No 45073**
Below left **Blackburn: 5MT 4-6-0 No 45464**
I always liked the name 'Garstang & Catterall', which, like other stations on this stretch of line between Preston and Lancaster, such as Bay Horse, had quite a ring to it. With the hills of the Trough of Bowland to your right as you went north, there was always a sense of anticipation that Grayrigg and Shap banks lay not so far ahead. The Class 5 is waiting in the bay platform for a down express to pass – the station closed on 3 February 1969.

At Blackburn the Class 5 is coasting into the very neat and tidy station with a local train for Preston.

Above right **Rose Grove: 4MT 4-6-0 No 75018, 1958**
Although of course I didn't know it when I took this picture, Rose Grove was destined to be one of the last centres of operational steam 10 years later. On a typically wet and gloomy Lancashire day, No 75018 pulls out of the station with a train for Skipton.

Below **Oxenholme: 9F 2-10-0**
On another pouring wet day, this time in the fells at Oxenholme, the 9F is gently easing forward before beginning the climb up Grayrigg bank with an empty coal train. The small rather than full-size signals at the end of the platform are for sighting purposes.

Above **Preston: 7F 0-8-0 No 49382**
The bank of the River Ribble at this point was a splendid vantage point to photograph trains crossing on the East Lancashire Railway bridge. In between its freight duties, the 'G2A' is bound for the station with a single brake-van. In the background are the two bridges carrying the West Coast Main Line over the river.

Above right **Warrington: 8F 2-8-0 No 48033**
Further south, the 8F is coming across the River Mersey with a coal train, a sight so commonplace in steam days that these trains were almost ignored in preference for the more glamorous expresses hauled by named locomotives. No 48033 was one of the more long-lived of the class, lasting until June 1968, two months from the end of steam.

Right **Clapham: 5MT 4-6-0 No 45374**
Although the Settle to Morecambe and Carnforth line (the 'Little North Western') lacked the glamour of the Settle & Carlisle, it could offer some attractive locations such as this viaduct over the River Wenning. The Class 5 is on a typical train from Leeds to Morecambe in June 1965.

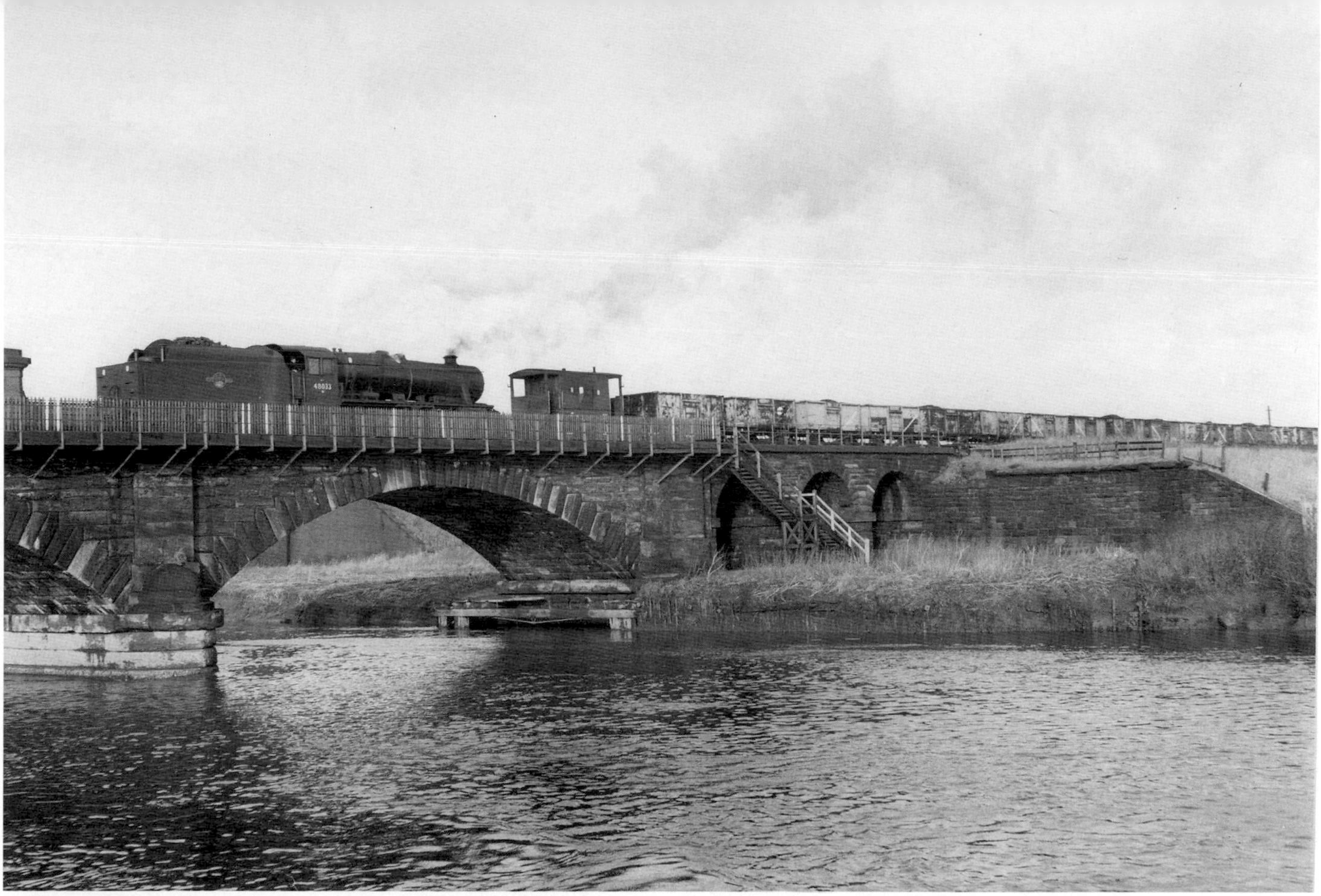

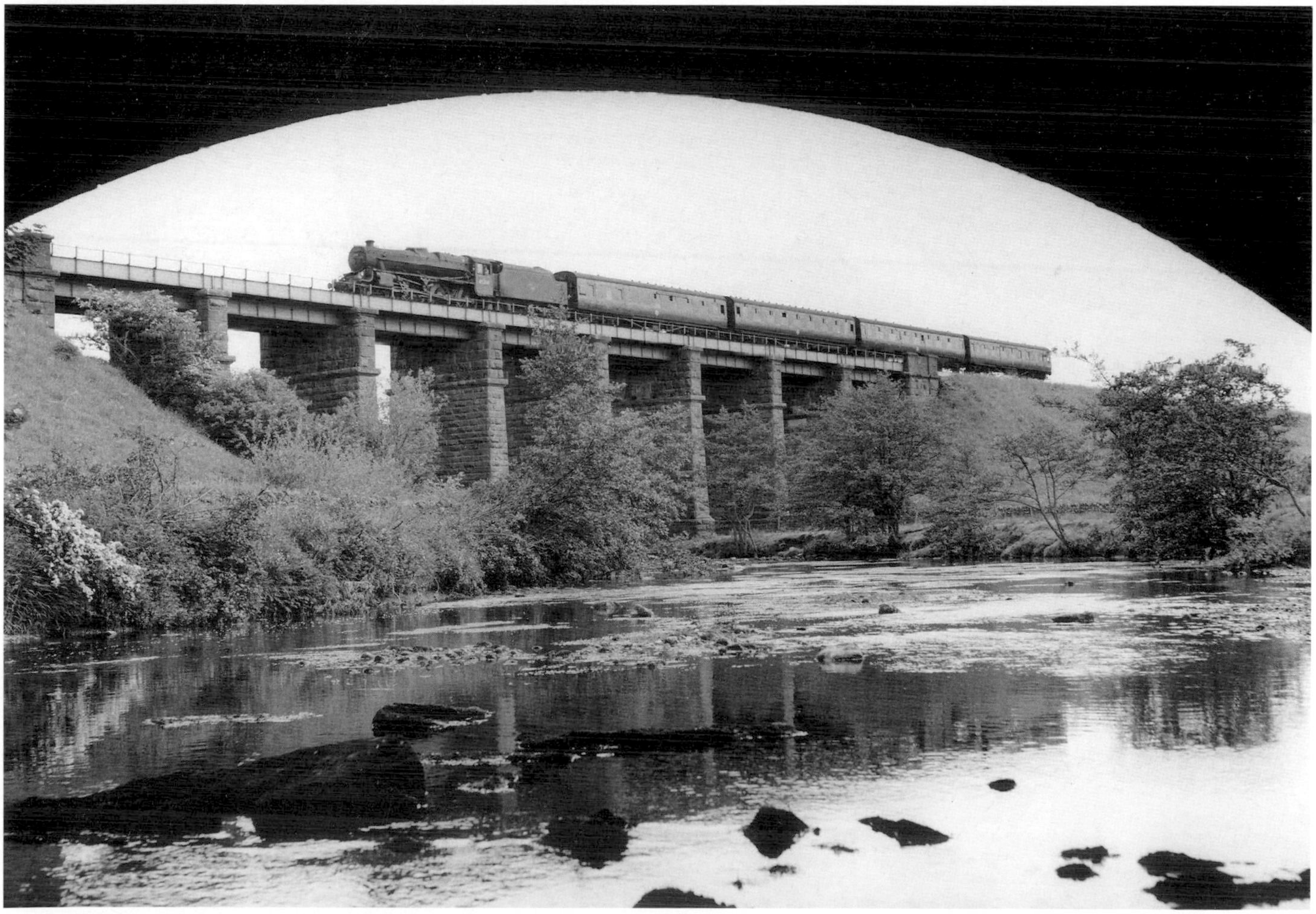

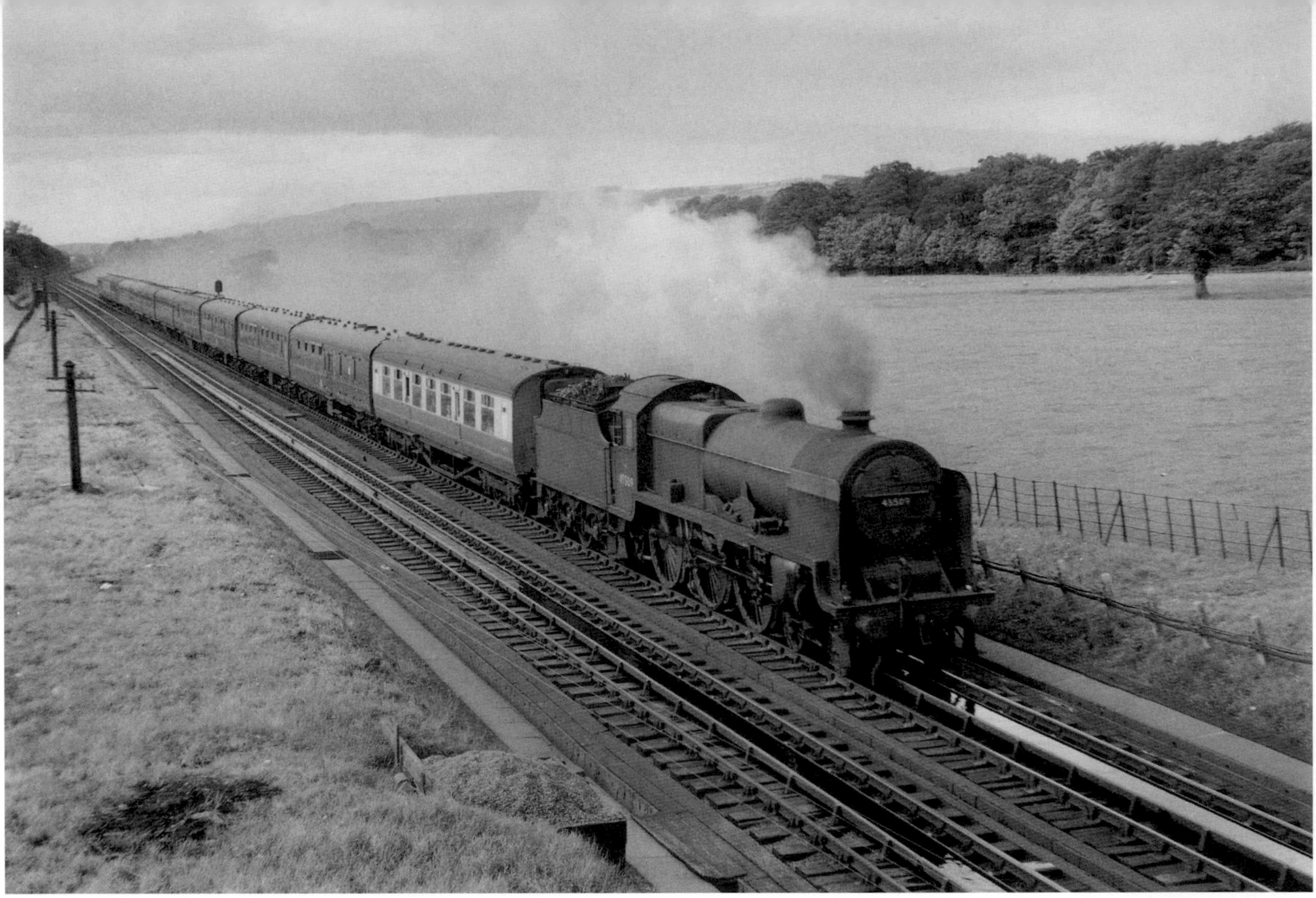

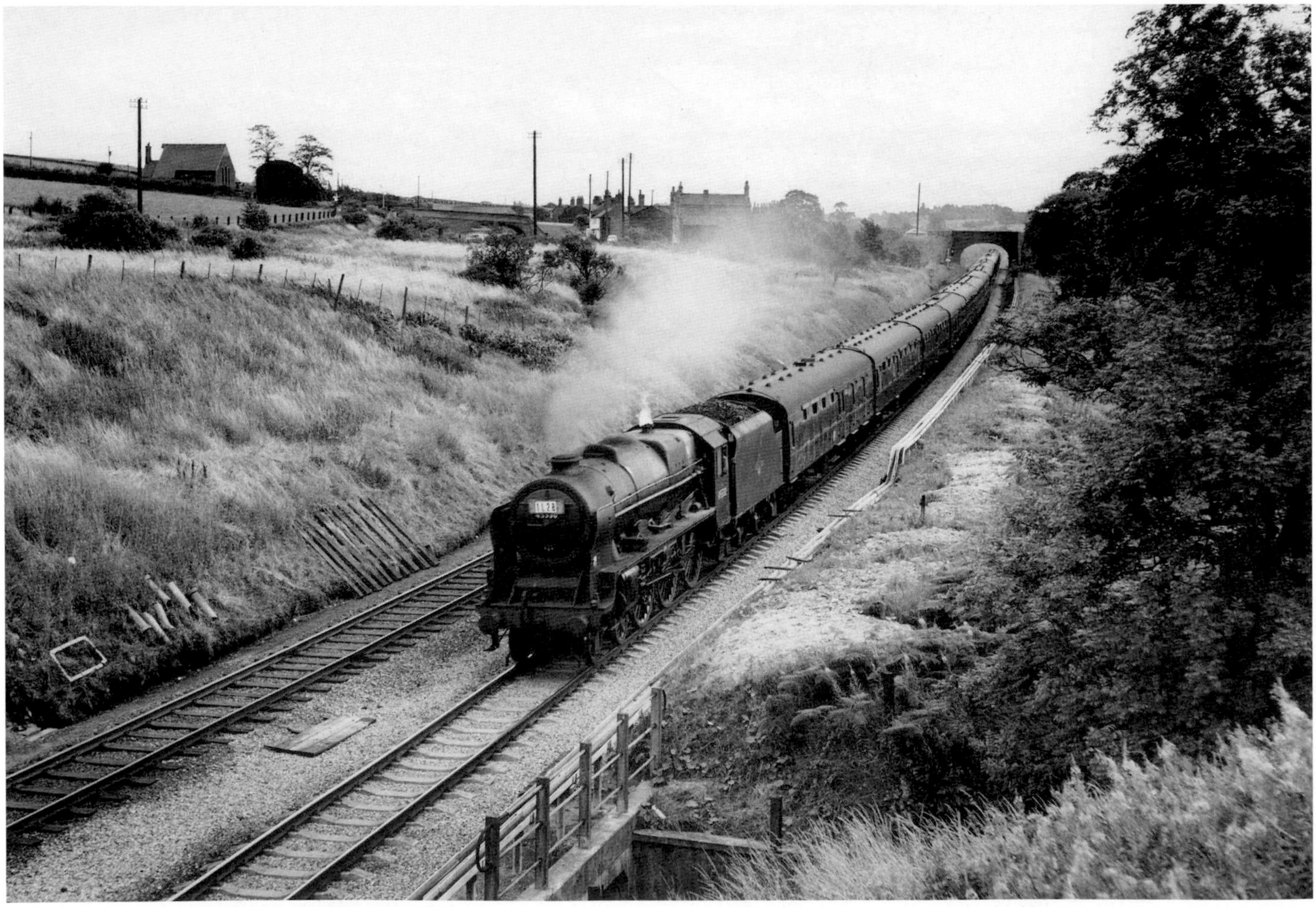

Above left Brock troughs: Unrebuilt 'Patriot' 4-6-0 No 45509 *The Derbyshire Yeomanry*, **Summer 1960**

The angular lines of the unrebuilt 'Patriots' were in direct contrast to the more modern appearance of their rebuilt sisters. No 45509 does not seem to have the need to take water from the troughs as its heads south towards Preston with a Manchester train, which has an Eastern Region Thompson-period coach behind the locomotive. At this time the unrebuilt engines were still hard at work on the main line, but of the London Midland Region's front-line passenger locomotives they were the first to go, as delivery of main-line diesel locomotives gained momentum. No 45509 was withdrawn in August 1961 from Newton Heath shed.

Below left Preston Brook: Rebuilt 'Patriot' 4-6-0 No 45530 *Sir Frank Ree*, **Summer 1963**

No 45530 is on a down Summer Saturday extra passing Preston Brook, where the Trent & Mersey and Bridgewater Canals run almost parallel to the railway. This rebuilt 'Patriot' was the last of the class in service, leading an almost charmed life, surviving on freight duties during the latter half of 1965 from its base at Carlisle (Upperby). The last three other remaining 7P locomotives were also so employed during this time – sister No 45531 *Sir Frederick Harrison*, and rebuilt 'Scots' Nos 46115 *Scots Guardsman* and 46140 *The King's Royal Rifle Corps*. But No 45530 outlived them all, lasting until December 1965.

Above Garstang & Catterall: Rebuilt 'Royal Scot' 4-6-0 No 46147 *The Northamptonshire Regiment*

When I took this picture the down bay platform was being used to berth permanent way wagons. Rebuilt 'Scot' No 46147 is heading south on this fine summer day in 1960 with an express for Euston. The locomotive was among the first of its class to be withdrawn in November 1962.

Below Tebay: Rebuilt 'Royal Scot' 4-6-0 No 46106 *Gordon Highlander*

This rebuilt 'Scot' was notable in that it was fitted with straight-sided smoke deflectors as used on BR Standard locomotives. It was withdrawn in December 1962. The locomotive has just passed Tebay station and is heading towards the water troughs at Dillicar.

Preston: 'Princess Coronation' 4-6-2 No 46231 *Duchess of Atholl*
The crème de la crème of West Coast Main Line motive power was of course the 'Duchess' Class, as the locomotives were popularly known. Here is a typical heavy 14-coach Anglo-Scottish express of the late 1950s/early 1960s leaving Preston for the south. You can almost hear the sharp bark of the big Stanier 'Pacific' at it accelerates the train towards Wigan and Crewe in the summer of 1960. It seemed that these magnificent locomotives would go on for ever, so it was almost unbelievable to read that, together with No 46232 *Duchess of Montrose*, No 46231 had been withdrawn in December 1962 from Polmadie shed, Glasgow, the first of the class to go.

Above **Dillicar troughs: 'Princess Coronation' 4-6-2 No 46244** *King George VI*
Particularly on a busy Summer Saturday, Dillicar was a delightfully quiet location to see and photograph the procession of trains that passed. No 46244 is heading north with what looks like a Summer Saturday extra. The locomotive was one of the last batch of the class in service, which were withdrawn en masse in October 1964 when they finally became surplus to requirements, due to the influx of the English Electric (Class 40) and Brush (Class 47) Type 4 diesels.

Below **Brock troughs: 'Princess Coronation' 4-6-2 No 46231** *Duchess of Atholl*
Here is No 46231 again, this time on rather more menial duties working a southbound vans train. *The Railway Observer* records that in their last year of operation the duties of the 'Duchesses' varied widely from main-line expresses to the ultimate indignity on 7 April 1964, when Crewe North's No 46235 *City of Birmingham* was seen working a train of up coal empties through Preston. The story ended happily for this locomotive, of course, as towards the end of 1965 it was taken into Crewe Works for restoration, repainted in BR lined green and sent to the Birmingham Museum of Science and Industry (now the Thinktank Birmingham Museum of Science). It remains there unchanged to this day.

Shap: 'Princess Coronation' 4-6-2 No 46236 *City of Bradford*

A lovely day in high summer sees this 'Duchess' steadily climbing the 1 in 75 gradient with an express for Glasgow composed of LMS stock. It is worth remembering that in 1961, when this photograph was taken, trains on weekdays like the 9.05am 'Royal Scot' from Euston did not arrive at Carlisle until 2.25pm and Glasgow Central at 4.15pm, a journey time of more than 7 hours. A slower train like the 9.50am from Euston took not far off 9 hours for the journey.

Docker Hall: 'Princess Coronation' 4-6-2 No 46256 *Sir William A. Stanier FRS*

With steam to spare, No 46256 is coming up Grayrigg bank in August 1961 with a northbound express. It is a great loss that this locomotive was not preserved. Built with detailed improvements under the regime of H. A. Ivatt at Crewe in 1947, this locomotive and its sister No 46257 *City of Salford* could always be easily recognised by their shortened cab sheets. It was scrapped in October 1964 and, together with seven other members of the class, sold to the Troon Shipbreaking Company in Ayrshire. A further ten went to J. Cashmore at Great Bridge. What a tragic sight they must have made at the scrapyards.

Shap: 'Princess Royal' 4-6-2 No 46212 *Duchess of Kent*
The 'Princess Royal' Class was somewhat overshadowed by its slightly bigger sisters, the 'Princess Coronations'. However, many regarded them as rather more impressive locomotives with their long slim-looking boilers and small chimneys. They were regular performers on the heavy Anglo-Scottish expresses like this one near Scout Green. No 46212 was withdrawn in October 1961 from Crewe North shed.

**Shap: 'Princess Royal' 4-6-2 No 46208 *Princess Helena Victoria*
and a 4MT 2-6-4T**

Crossing the infant River Lune at Greenholme, another smartly turned-out 'Princess Royal' is forging northward with an Anglo-Scottish train, which has an ex-GWR 'Siphon' van behind the locomotive. At the extreme right of the upper picture you can just see the smoke from the banker, which in this case is a Fowler 2-6-4T. Towards the end of their career the 'Princess Royals' spent much of their time in store, often only being returned to steam to help out during busy holiday periods. However, because they were withdrawn slightly earlier than the 'Princess Coronations' they tended not to suffer the indignity of being used on menial freight duties, like a duchess being reduced to a scullery maid! No 46208 was one of the last of the class to be withdrawn in October 1962.

Oxenholme: 4MT 2-6-4T No 42095

The various varieties of 2-6-4T were long a welcome feature of the railway scene in the North West and were employed on a range of duties. This Fairburn tank, built at Brighton in 1951, is on banking work at Oxenholme, assisting freight trains up Grayrigg. It is about to buffer up to the brake-van, where the guard seems to have a nice fire going in his stove judging by the smoke from its chimney. Final steam banking duties were performed by Standard 4MT 4-6-0s, including No 75027, now based at the Bluebell Railway, and finished in May 1968.

Right **Cherry Tree: 4MT 2-6-4T No 42569**
Cherry Tree station was situated 2 miles or so west of
Blackburn, and No 42569 is calling with a typical
Lancashire local train from Accrington to Preston. This
Stanier two-cylinder locomotive was withdrawn in
January 1964, and sadly none of the 2-6-4Ts lasted until
the end of steam, the final ones going towards the end of
1967.

Below **Brock troughs: 4MT 2-6-4T No 42119**
This Fairburn tank has no need of the watering facilities
as it speeds south with a seven-coach up local from
Lancaster. The train is comprised of mostly main-line
stock but there is a strengthening ex-LMS compartment
coach behind the locomotive.

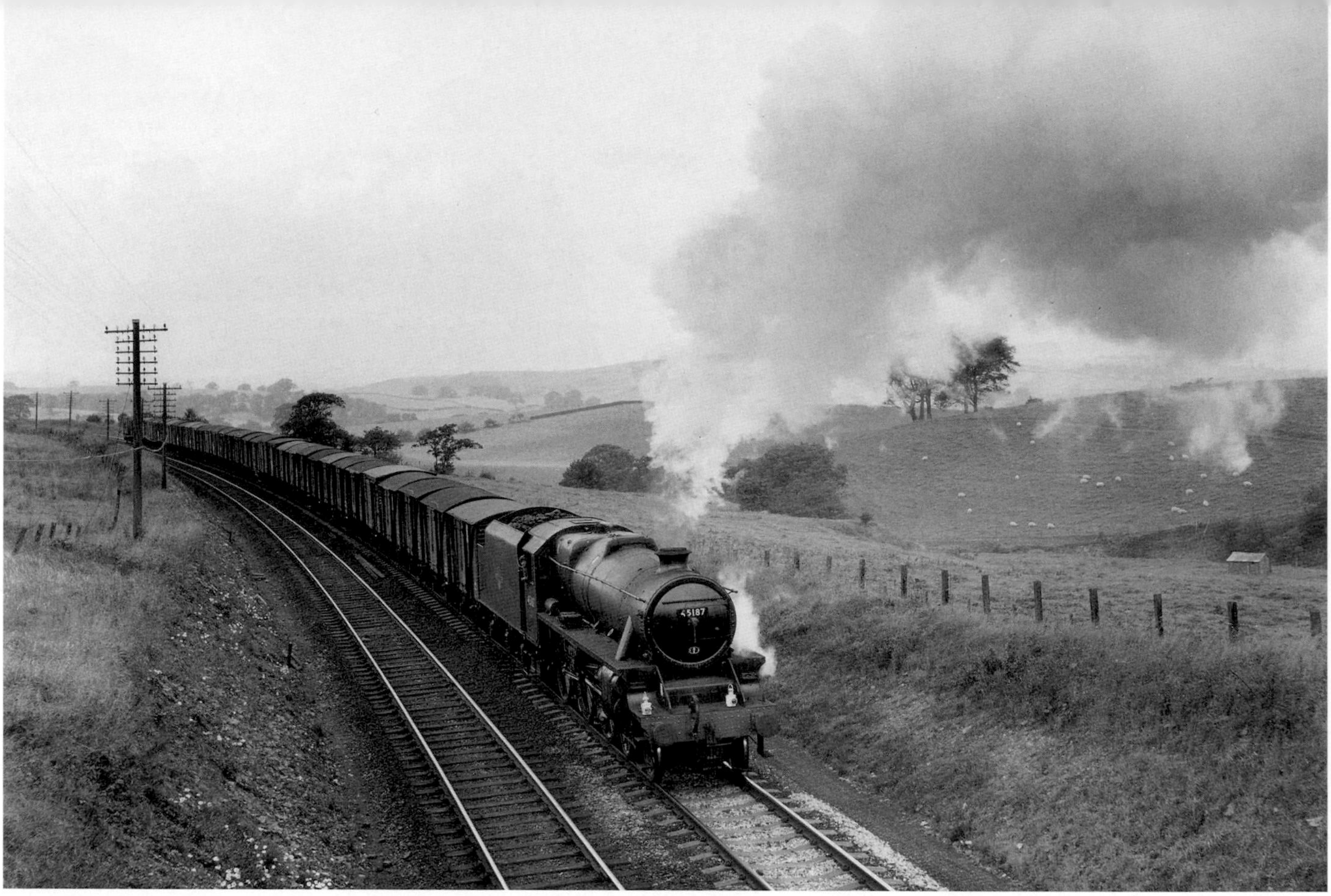
45187

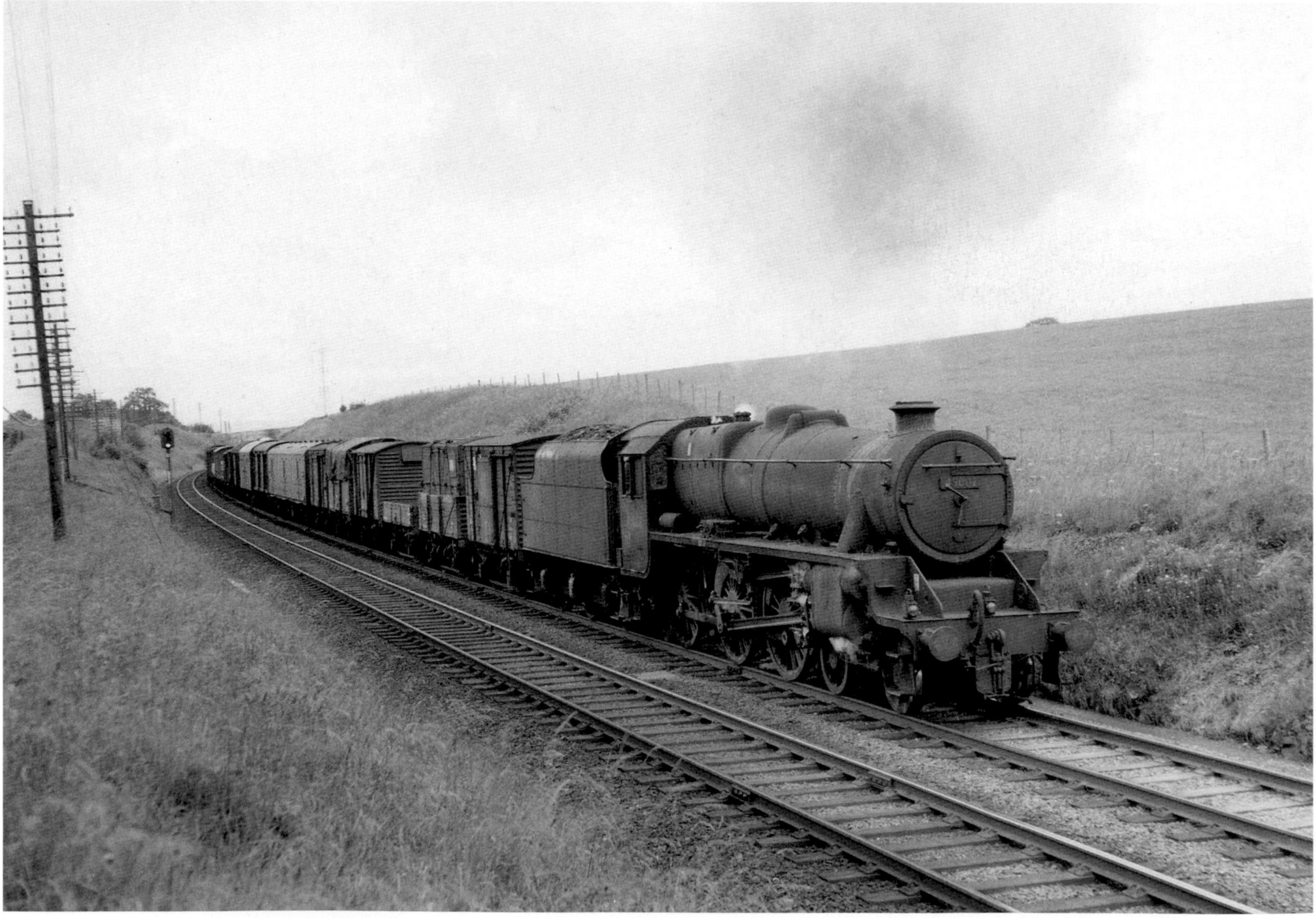

Left **Hardrigg: 5MT 4-6-0 No 45187**
Below left **Docker Hall: 5MT 4-6-0 No 45002**
Below **Grayrigg loop: 9F 2-10-0 No 92154**
Here are three pictures showing freight trains on Grayrigg bank. Though not as steep as Shap, it came at the end of a long 13-mile northbound climb that began just before Milnthorpe. Nos 45187 and 45002 are on fitted freights for Carlisle, while Speke Junction's 9F is leaving the up siding at Grayrigg with a train of steel ingots. Note the

gradient post on the left-hand side of the picture, and the fine LNWR signals controlling the siding. No 92154 was one of a batch of 9Fs built at Crewe in 1957. A further 30 followed in 1958, including No 92250, the last of the 7,331 locomotives to be built at Crewe. As noted in the Introduction it left the Works after a special ceremony on 15 December but was destined only to last until December 1965 – what a waste of a fine locomotive! The 9Fs also did not quite make the end of steam, the last one, No 92167, being withdrawn at the end of June 1968.

Above Winwick: 'Britannia' 4-6-2 No 70035 (formerly *John Milton*)
Below Docker Hall: 'Britannia' 4-6-2 No 70000 (formerly *Britannia*)
Above right Grayrigg: 'Britannia' 4-6-2 No 70049 *Solway Firth*
Below right Grayrigg loop: 'Britannia' 4-6-2 No 70016 (formerly *Ariel*)
Despite being in a run-down condition, the 'Britannias' still retained something of their old charisma even though the nameplates were removed towards the end of their life. From working fast expresses on the Norwich to Liverpool Street line when it was new in 1952, No 70035 is demoted to freight train duties. On a dull winter afternoon it is approaching Winwick Junction with a northbound train.

Climbing Grayrigg bank on a northbound local, No 70000 looks in even worse condition, with a badly leaking front end.

Coming down Grayrigg bank from the north in the summer of 1961, Newton Heath's No 70049 is on a Glasgow to Manchester and Liverpool train. Its solid-looking BR1D tender gives the locomotive a more powerful appearance.

Finally, No 70016 is passing Grayrigg loop sidings with an up parcels train while a 9F waits in the loop to proceed (see page 53). *Ariel* spent most of its early years on the Western Region but was transferred to the London Midland in 1961.

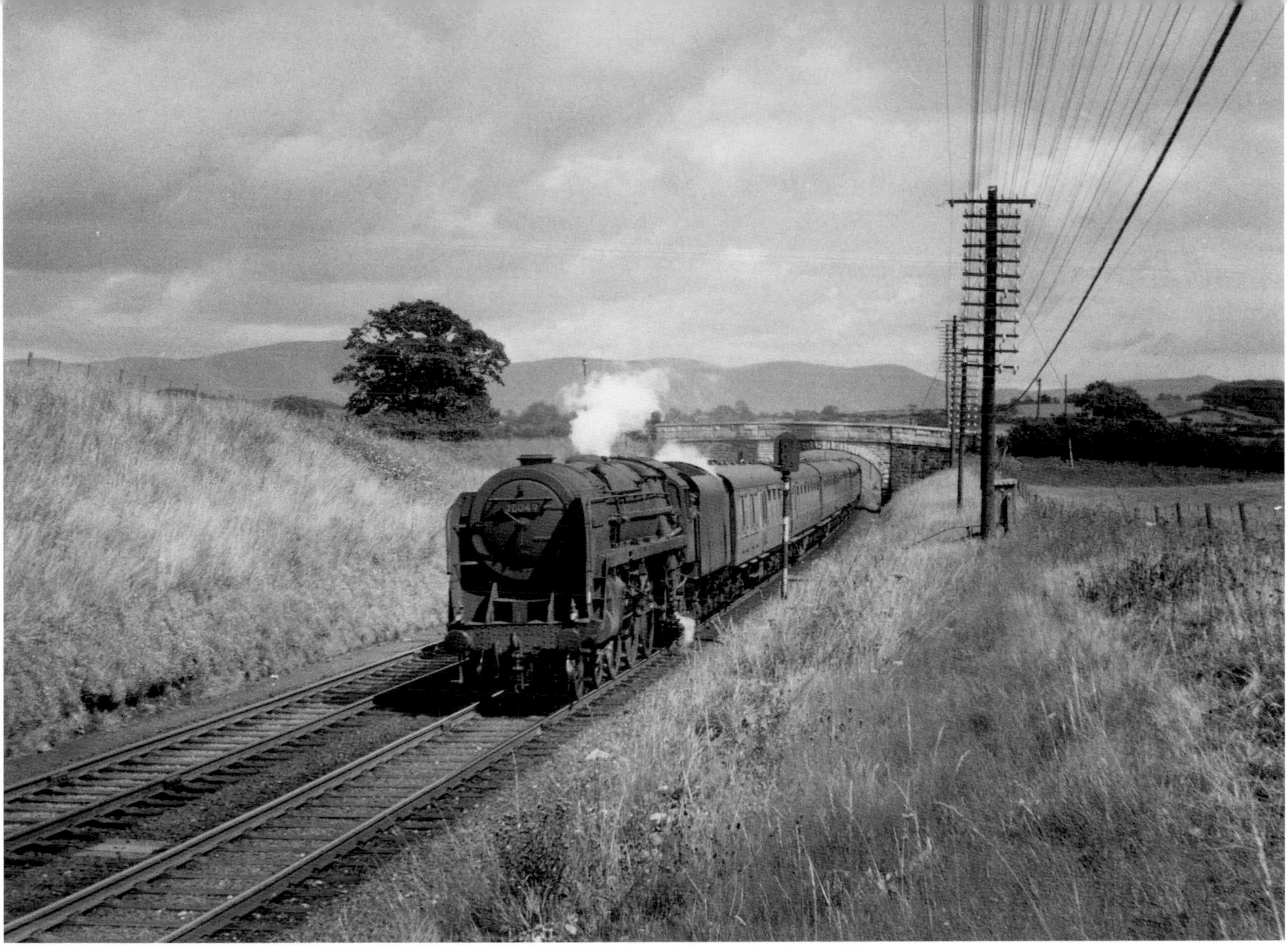

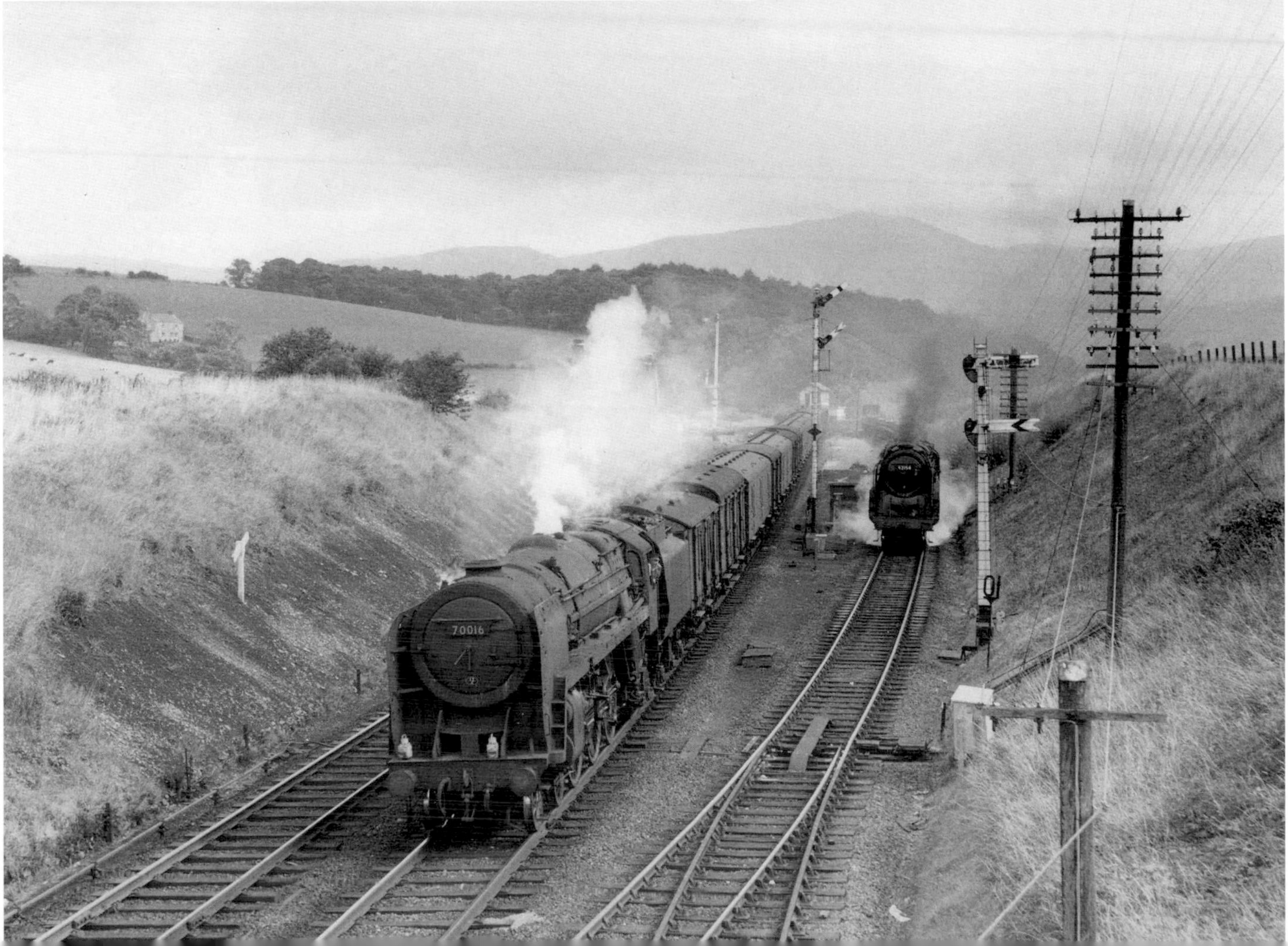

70016

Above **Shap: 'Clan' 4-6-2 No 72004** *Clan Macdonald*
Above right **Low Gill: 'Clan' 4-6-2 No 72003** *Clan Fraser*
Right **Settle Junction: 'Clan' 4-6-2 No 72007 (formerly** *Clan Mackintosh***)**
At the bottom of the pile of 'Pacifics' on the West Coast Main Line were the 'Clans', which never quite seemed to fulfil their promise, though they did some useful work on Glasgow to Manchester and Liverpool line trains. Judging by the pall of black smoke, No 72004 seems to have its work cut out lifting this train of 12 ex-LMS coaches up the bank in the summer of 1959, despite being assisted in the rear by a 2-6-4T.

No 72003 is having an easier time coasting through the platforms of the closed Low Gill station with a southbound train.

Latterly the 'Clans' were employed on stopping trains over the S&C, such as this northbound service behind a very neglected-looking No 72007, which has lost its nameplates. Nos 72003 and 72004 were early withdrawals in December 1962, while No 72007 survived until December 1965, the last member of the class in use.

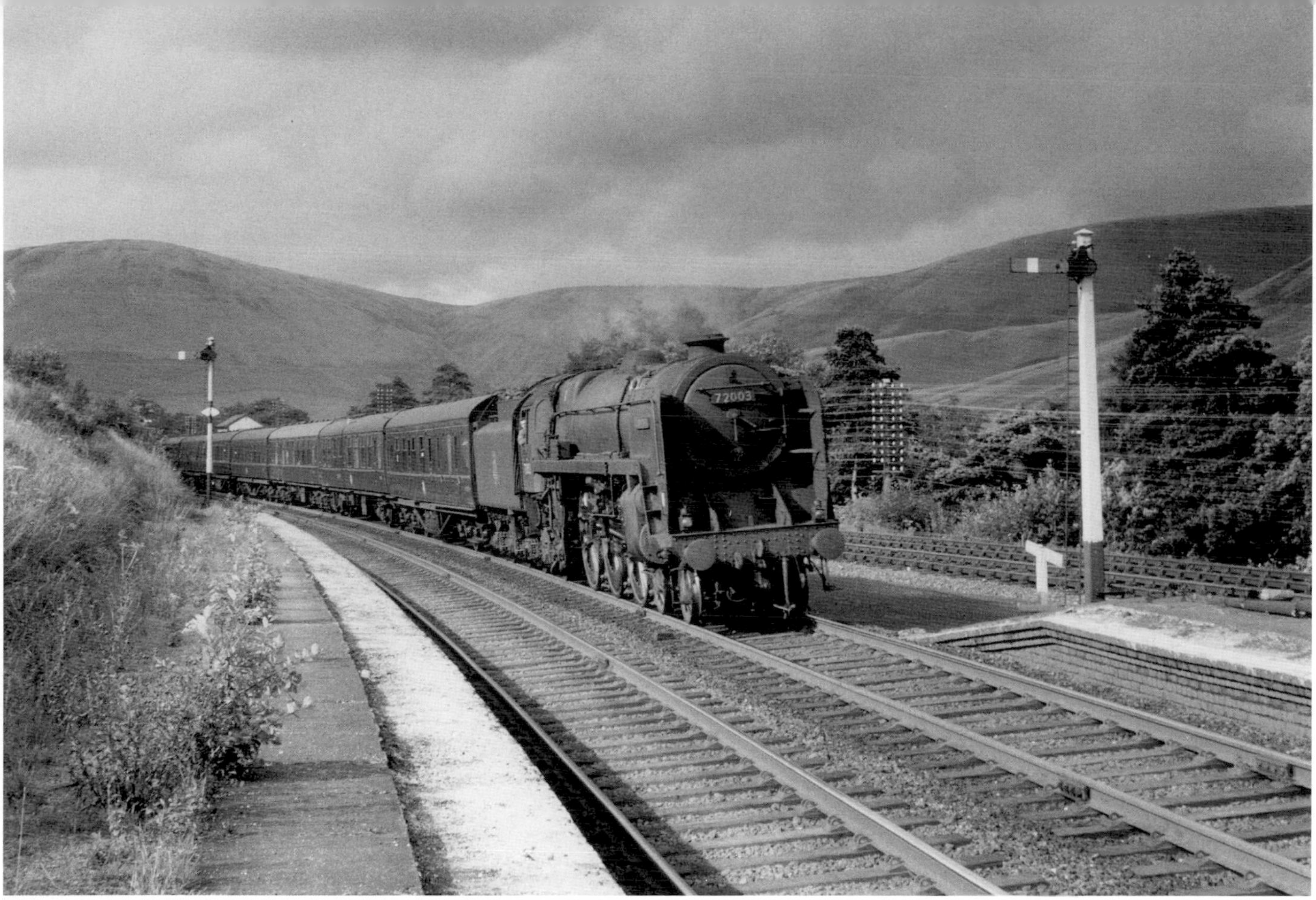
72003

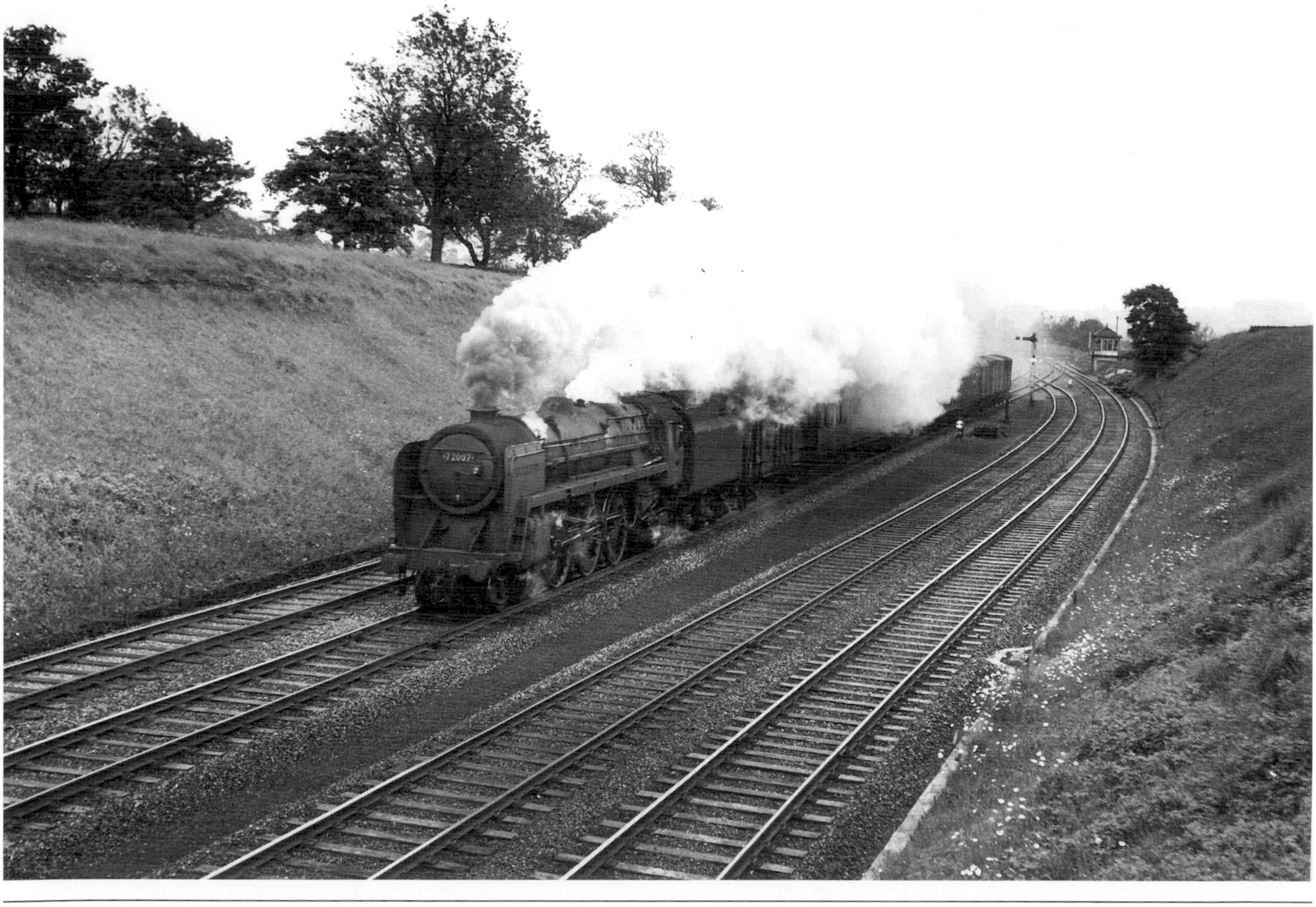
72007

Above **Euxton: 4F 0-6-0 No 44568**
Below **Greenodd: 4F 0-6-0 No 44487**

While normally used on freight workings, the 4Fs could occasionally be seen stretching their legs on Summer extra trains when requirements for motive power were at their greatest. Despite the coating of grime on it, No 44568 looks as if it has recently had a general overhaul, which is why it may have been picked for this train, possibly bound for Blackpool.

There were regular excursion trains up the picturesque branch from Ulverston to Lakeside (Windermere), such as this one with Barrow shed's No 44487, which is crossing the River Leven at Greenodd on a working from Lakeside in the summer of 1961.

***Above* Haverthwaite: 5MT 4-6-0 No 44944**
Below* Lakeside: 'Jubilee' 4-6-0 No 45633 *Aden
Excursions to Lakeside were more usually hauled by larger locomotives than 4Fs, such as the Class 5 seen here leaving Haverthwaite. In the background a Midland '2F' 0-6-0 is on the local pick-up goods.

At Lakeside in August 1961 the 'Jubilee' is arriving at the station with a train of very mixed stock including an ex-GWR coach. The locomotive will have run round its train at Ulverston. Excursion traffic ran until 3 September 1965.

Above **Arnside Viaduct: 4MT 4-6-0 and 5MT 4-6-0**

Against the background of the fells the two locomotives bring a southbound train over the long viaduct. The two GUVs at the rear of the train are separated from the rest of the formation by a brake-van. The viaduct over the River Kent has 50 piers and is 522 yards long.

Below **Ravenglass: 5MT 4-6-0 No 45383 and 4MT 2-6-4T**

This pair of locomotives have just arrived with a train from Workington to Barrow-in-Furness and the south composed of ex-LMS stock. On the extreme right of the picture a train is waiting to depart on the Ravenglass & Eskdale Railway. Glimpsed above the Class 5 in the goods yard are two Pullman cars used as Camping Coaches.

Above **Haverthwaite: 2F 0-6-0 No 58177**
Quite apart from the excursion traffic to Lakeside, there was a regular goods service on the branch from Ulverston worked at this time by Johnson 0-6-0s shedded at Barrow, far from their usual ex-Midland Railway haunts. In July 1961 the locomotive is pausing between shunting duties while the fireman appears to be looking at the injector pipe. By April 1962 the Johnson 0-6-0s had been put into store at Barrow and were withdrawn later in the year. The freight working was taken over by more modern locomotives such as Ivatt Class 2 2-6-0s until the last day of working on 21 April 1967.

Below **Near Cark & Cartmel: 4F 0-6-0 No 44399**
In July 1961 the 4F is heading towards Carnforth with a pick-up goods from Barrow, the haphazard variety of wagons in the train being typical of the time. No 44399 was withdrawn in February 1964 from Trafford Park (9E) shed.

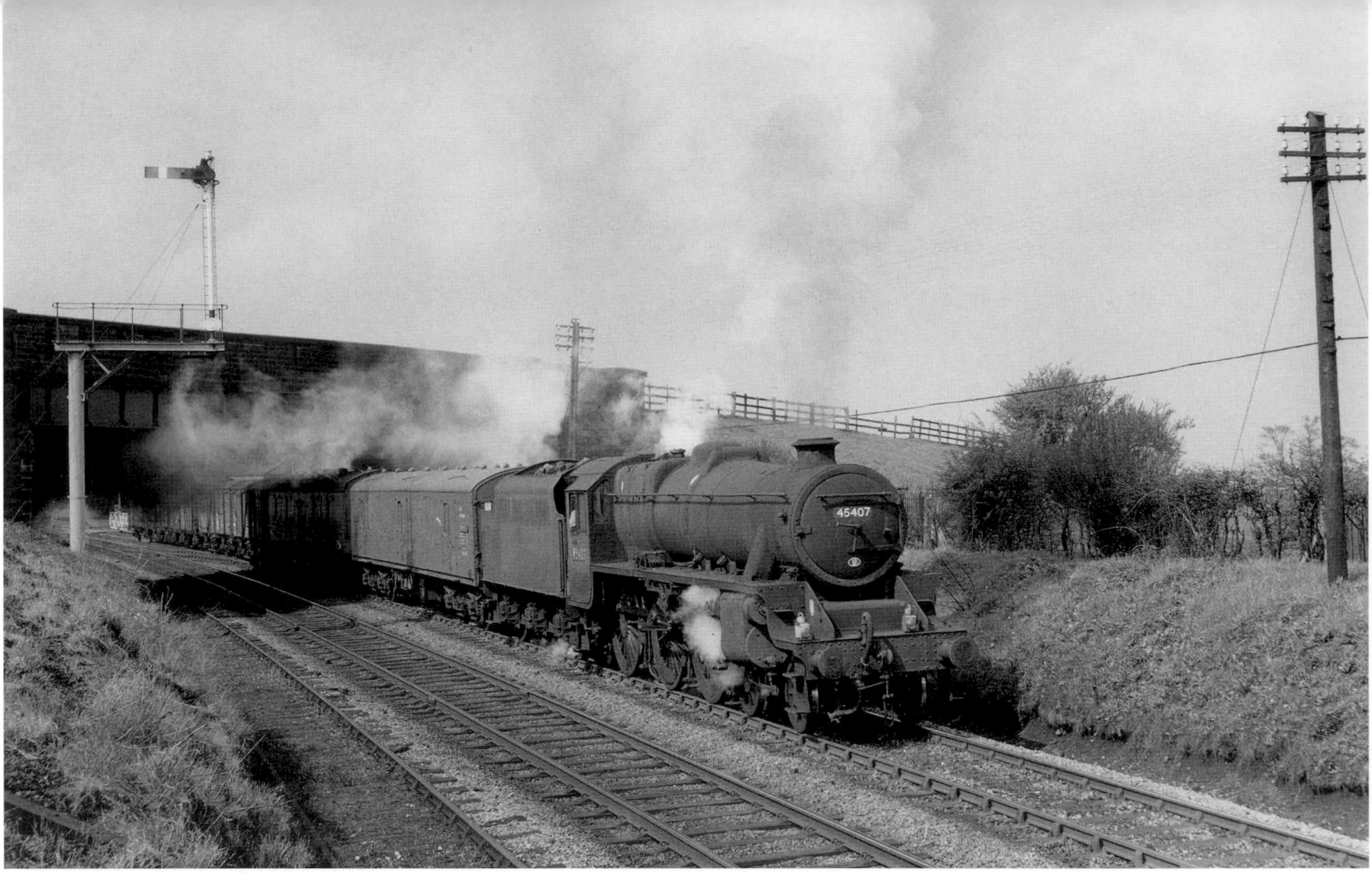
45407

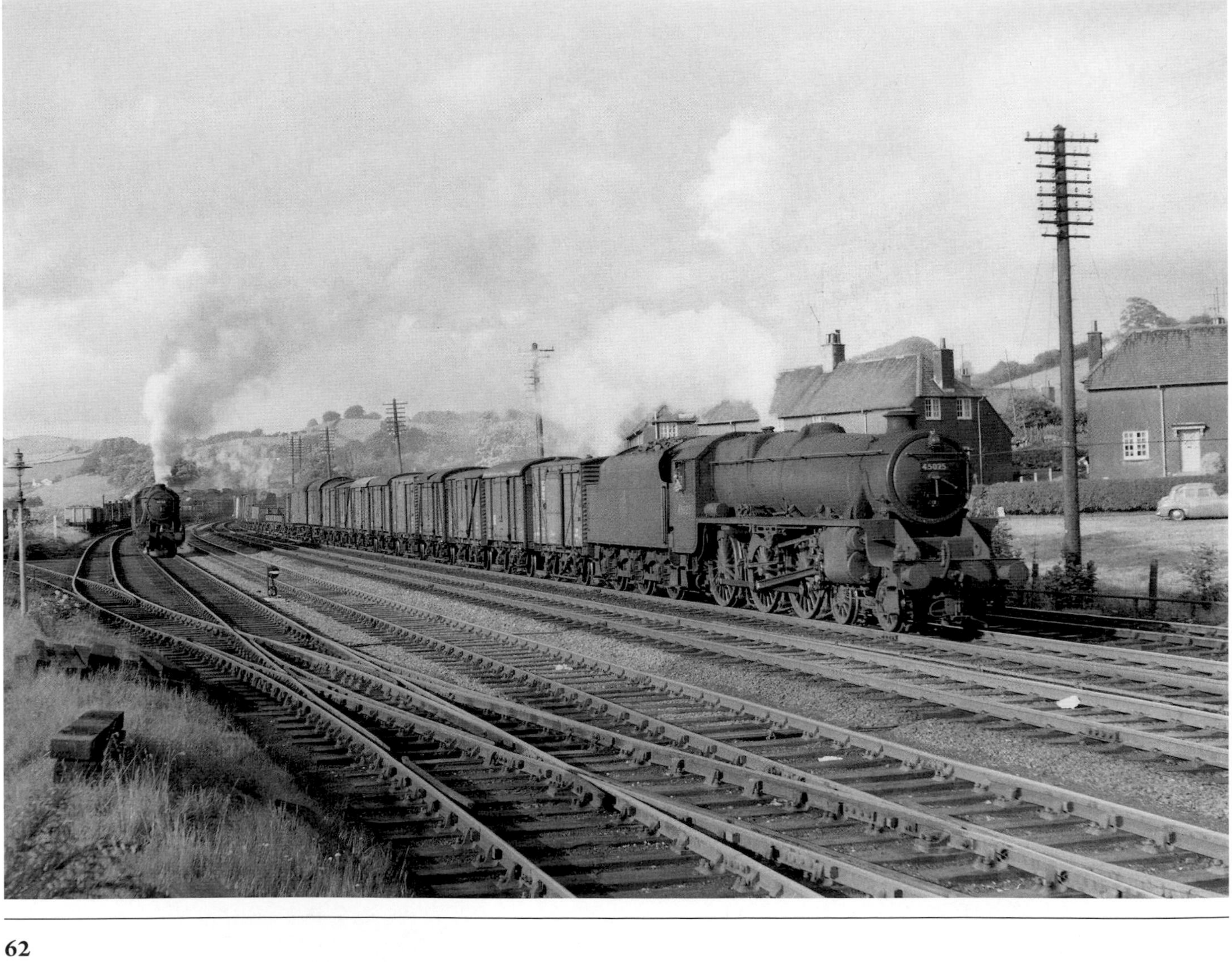

Left **Near Bentham: 5MT 4-6-0 No 45407**
The locomotives depicted on this page and the next
have one thing in common – they all escaped cutting up
and are still with us. No 45407, based today on the East
Lancashire Railway, is on a parcels train from
Morecambe to Leeds. It lasted right to the end of steam
in August 1968 and, like No 45025, was used on the 4th
(see page 127).

Below left **Oxenholme: 5MT 4-6-0 No 45025**
On a fine summer evening No 45025 is pulling away
from Oxenholme with a freight train for the south. It
later had its moment of fame when it worked the last up
'Belfast Boat Train' from Heysham to Manchester
Victoria on 5 May 1968 – see page 122.

Above right **Near Daresbury: 5MT 2-6-0 No 42765**
Apart from No 42700 at the 'Locomotion' Museum at Shildon and No 42859, which
is awaiting restoration, this is the only other Hughes 'Crab' to be preserved. Working
from Springs Branch (Wigan) shed, it is on a freight for Chester on 28 December
1963. It was withdrawn in December 1966 and went to Woodham's scrapyard at
Barry, but was rescued in April 1978. Today it is based at the East Lancashire Railway.

Below **Near Kirkby Stephen East: 4MT 2-6-0 No 43106**
No 43106 was withdrawn from Lostock Hall shed in June 1968, the only survivor of
this class of 162 locomotives. It had been used on the Midland & Great Northern line
in the late 1950s and had it not found its way to Lostock Hall shed, where steam hung
on to the very end, it might not have been saved to run again at the Severn Valley
Railway. Here it is working a freight to Merrygill Quarry in June 1965 on the line from
Appleby East, which was closed to passengers in 1962.

Above Near Daresbury: 8F 2-8-0 No 48502
Below **Shap: 5MT 4-6-0 No 45397**

Oil tank traffic was important in the North West with large refineries at Stanlow and Ellesmere Port. On a foggy winter morning the 8F has a number of oil tankers in its train as it heads west. Meanwhile, on Shap this heavily loaded oil train, protected from the locomotive by a brake-van and two wagons, needs banking assistance up the 1 in 75 gradient.

Near Galgate, south of Lancaster: '8F' 2-8-0
As a herd of Friesian cows is driven along the lane to the farm for milking, an 8F passes
by with a northbound vans train.

Norton: 5MT 4-6-0, 27 December 1965
On this freezing cold day, as the sun begins to set, a Class 5 heads past the closed
station towards Warrington with a train for Manchester.

Warrington: 5MT 4-6-0, 29 December 1965
Two days later the weather has remained settled enough for me to take this photograph of a Class 5 on the climb out of Bank Quay station to cross the Manchester Ship Canal. In the foreground the murky waters of the River Mersey slowly make their way towards Liverpool.

Wigan North Western: 5MT 4-6-0
Outlined against the golden western sky one cold winter afternoon, this Class 5 is
slowly pulling out of the station with a goods train for Preston.

Whelley loop line, Wigan: 8F 2-8-0
The battered fence in the foreground, made out of old sleepers, frames the 8F on a
local goods working, which is crossing the West Coast Main Line not far south of
Springs Branch.

Above **Patricroft shed: 5MT 4-6-0 No 73050**
Left **Edge Hill shed: 8F 2-8-0 No 48168**
All is quiet in the old shed at Patricroft as No 73050 rests amongst the sunlight and shadows. At Edge Hill the 8F still keeps steam alive at this once top link depot, but its heyday years are long past.

Above **Lostock Hall shed: 8F 2-8-0s**
Right **Bolton shed: 5MT 4-6-0**
Darkening clouds gather at Lostock Hall as these two
8Fs await their fate on the scrap road. At Bolton the
motion of the Class 5 has been severed ready for it to be
towed away for cutting up.

Left **Rose Grove shed: 5MT 4-6-0 No 45156**
***Ayrshire Yeomanry*, 2 August 1968**
Below **Ais Gill Viaduct: 5MT 4-6-0s Nos 44781 and 44871, 11 August 1968**

By then something of a celebrity locomotive, No 45156 is back at the shed after completing its last turn of duty on a freight working up to Clitheroe. However, on 4 August it was again very much in action on the train depicted on page 125. What a pity this named Class 5 was not saved.

On Sunday 11 August 1968, a week after the official end of steam, British Rail ran its own 'farewell' tour, 1T57 – as their tour brochure proclaimed at the time, 'British Rail runs out of Steam'. The cost for the 314-mile journey was 15 guineas (£15.75), which at the time was regarded as being outrageously expensive (but it did include refreshments). To put this figure in context, typical rail tour fares at this time were in the region of £2 to £4. The BR train left Liverpool Lime Street at 9.10am for Manchester Victoria; it then ran to Carlisle and back via the S&C, returning to Liverpool Lime Street at 7.50pm. I didn't see the train so this picture was taken by my friend Roger Cruse, who photographed the two immaculately turned-out Class 5s that worked from Carlisle to Manchester Victoria.

Above **Clapham (Yorks): 4MT 4-6-0 No 75044**
Below **High Bentham: 8F 2-8-0 and Type 2 Bo-Bo diesel**

No 75044 is coming through the station with a short oil train from Heysham. Note milepost 242 on the station building, the distance over the Midland Railway route to St Pancras. In the background the line to Ingleton and Low Gill goes straight ahead.

At High Bentham in June 1968 this train is probably the heavy Heysham to Neville Hill oil tank train, which was worked by an 8F plus a Type 2 (later Class 24) diesel towards the end of the steam era.

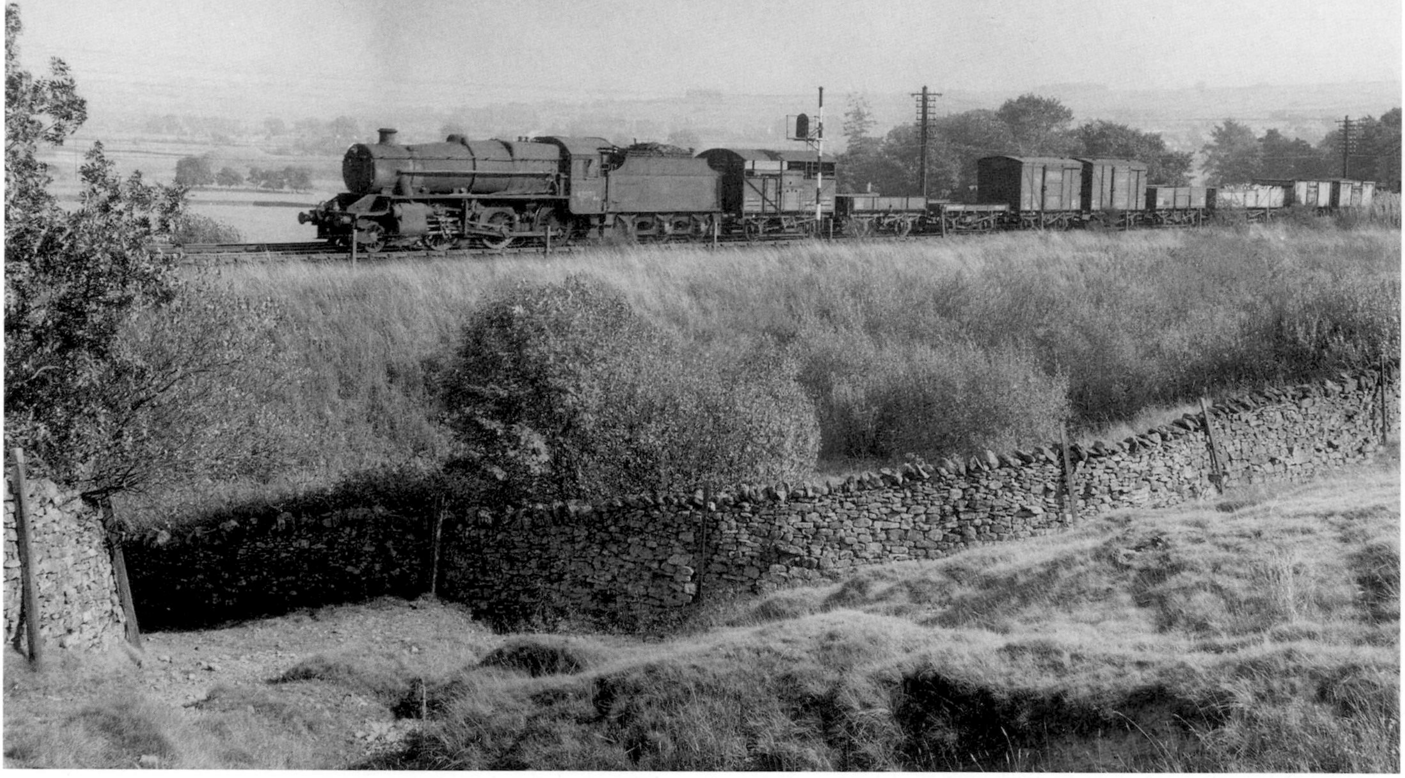

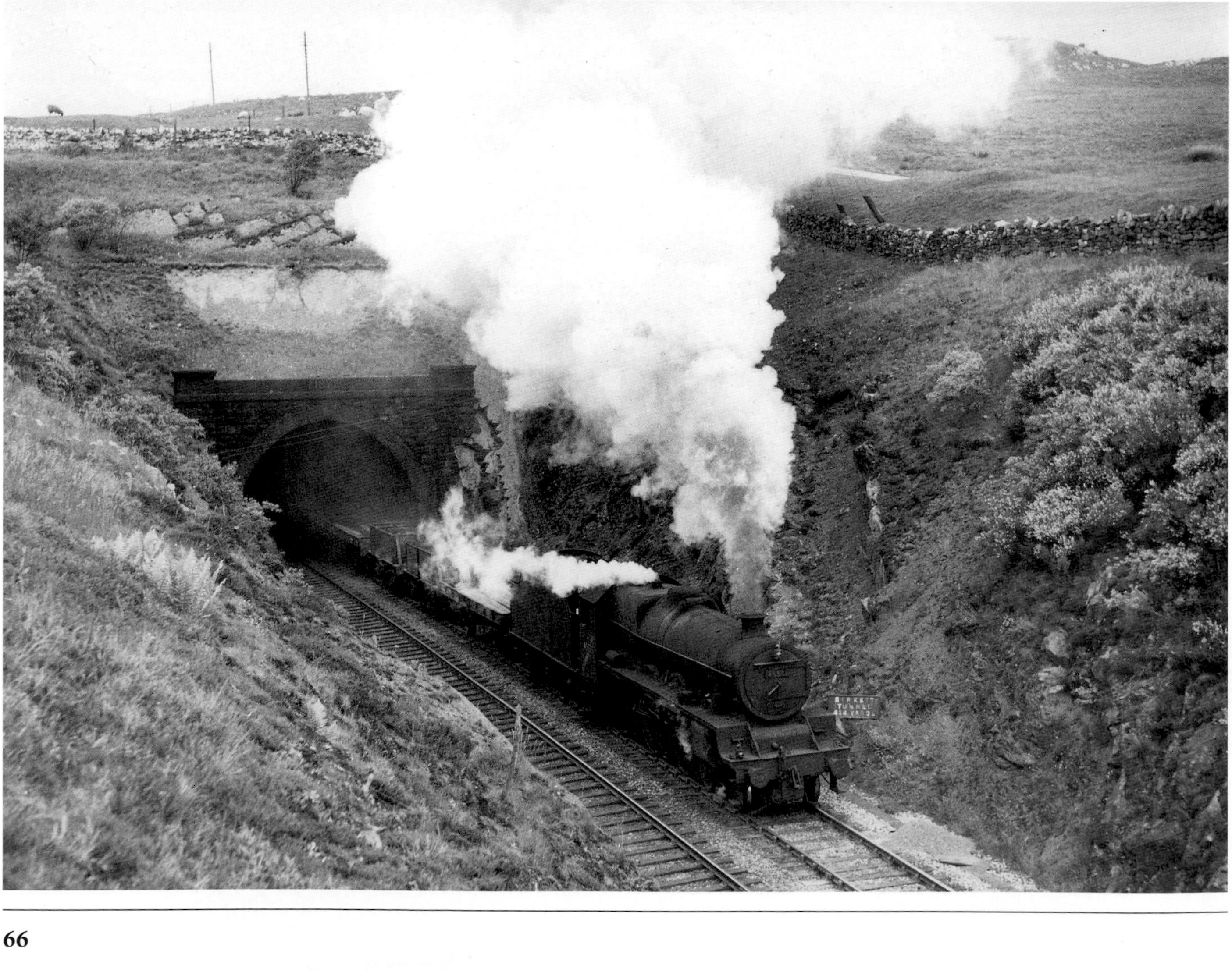
BIRKETT
TUNNEL

Left **Shap: 5MT 2-6-0 No 42979**
Below left **Birkett Tunnel: 'Jubilee' 4-6-0 No 45573**
Newfoundland
The Stanier 2-6-0s lasted until 1967, though most of the 40 had gone by the end of 1965, including No 42979, which was withdrawn in December 1964. Near the beginning of the climb up Shap it is being given a helping hand up the bank by a Fowler 2-6-4T. The post of the electric colour-light Distant signal is painted black and white to make it more visible.

The days when Leeds (Holbeck) shed's No 45573 worked the prestigious 'Waverley' and 'Thames-Clyde Express' are long since past. Looking in very shabby condition, it is emerging from the smoky 434-yard bore of Birkett Tunnel with a southbound freight. It carries the diagonal yellow stripe on the cab side, which I refer to on page 35.

This page **Preston Brook: 'Jubilee' 4-6-0s Nos 45595 *Southern Rhodesia* and 45655 *Keith***
I think this pair of photographs illustrate quite graphically the run-down of London Midland Region front-line motive power as the steam era drew to a close. In the summer of 1963 Crewe North shed's smartly turned-out No 45595 is at the head of an up Saturday extra. In contrast, near the end of its career a very neglected-looking *Keith*, disfigured with a yellow cab-side stripe, has been reduced to working this lowly-looking local freight, which includes an old sludge tender. No 45655 lasted three months longer than No 45595, being withdrawn in April 1965 from Warrington shed.

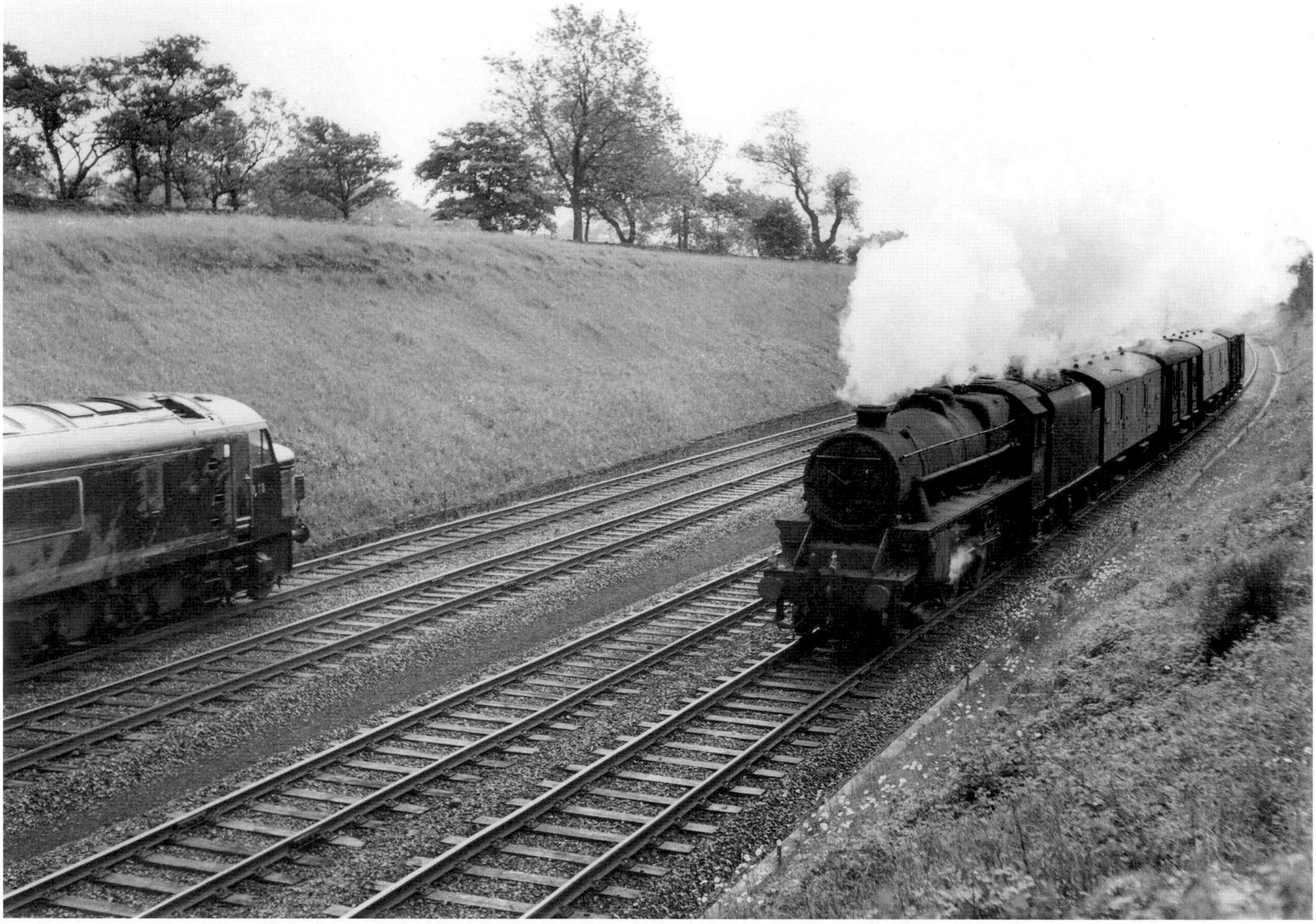

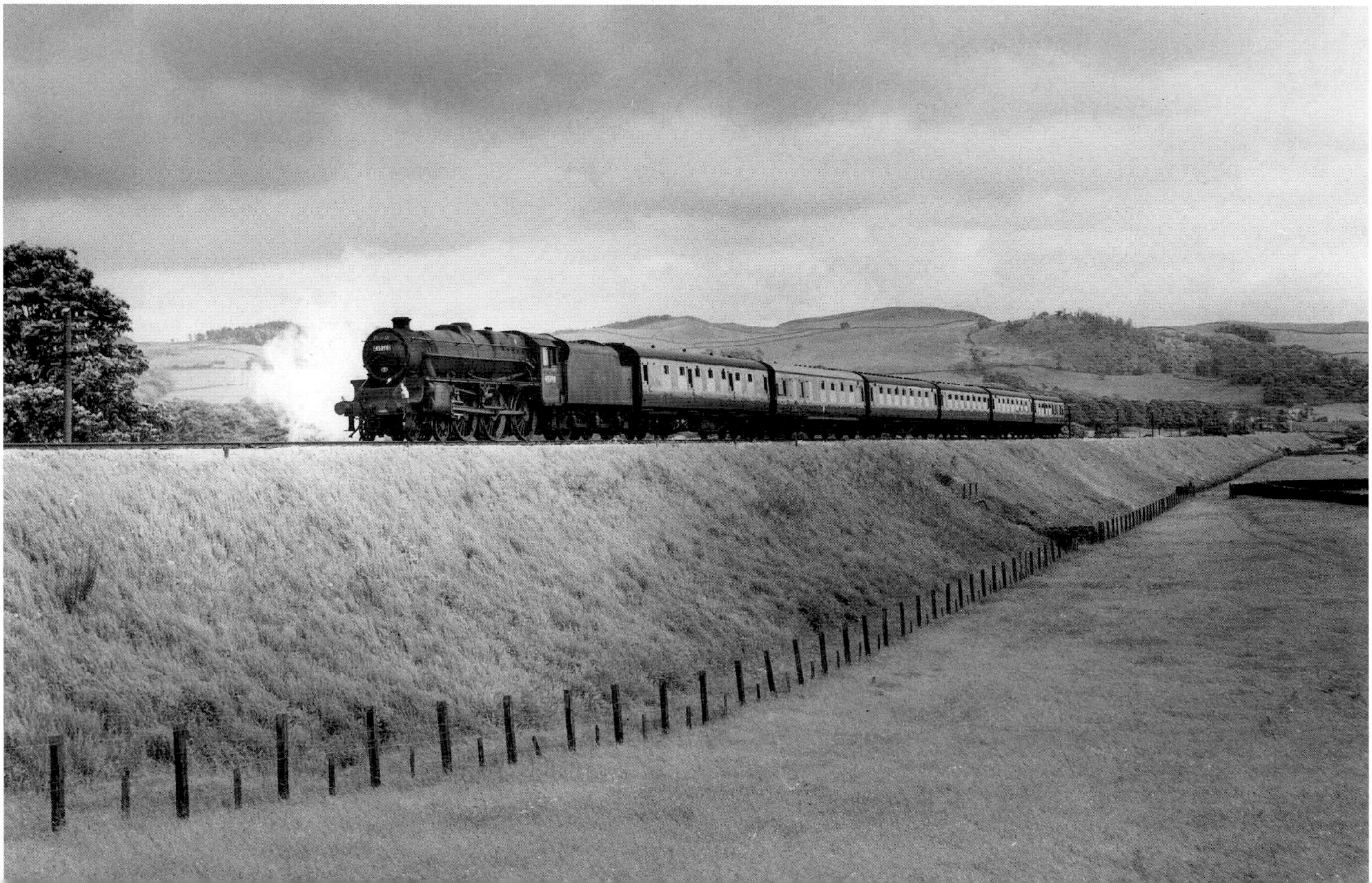

Left **Settle Junction: 'Peak' Type 4 and 5MT 4-6-0**
Down at Settle Junction, a Class 5 is heading towards Clapham on the Morecambe line with a vans train, while the dirty-looking diesel goes south with a train on the S&C line.

Opposite below **Near Giggleswick: 5MT 4-6-0 No 45390**
After turning away from the S&C at Settle Junction, the line to Carnforth and Morecambe runs through pleasant rolling countryside, as shown in this photograph of No 45390 in June 1965 just east of Giggleswick station, on a train composed of ex-LMS stock. The locomotive was destined to last until the end of steam shedded at Carnforth (10A).

Above **Settle Junction: 4MT 4-6-0 No 75057**
Here is a wider view of the junction, where No 75057 is coasting past me with a freight from the Clapham line. In the distance the S&C climbs away towards the hills on a 1 in 100 gradient, a sight that must have been quite daunting for the crew of a badly steaming locomotive on a heavy train.

Right **Hellifield: 5MT 4-6-0 No 44799**
The Class 5 is busy marshalling its freight, but the station and shed yard are looking desolate compared to the scene depicted on pages 16 and 17. The side of the locomotive shed, where once a 2P stood ready to assist trains over the S&C, can be seen on the extreme left of the picture. *The Railway Observer* graphically recorded of Hellifield in 1963 that, 'Apart from the few local passengers, little more than the wind now remains, howling as ever through this most windswept of all the Midland's windswept junction stations.' Happily the station building is now listed and has been restored.

***Above* Latchford: 9F 2-10-0**

On the LNWR line from Ditton Junction to Skelton Junction, Latchford station lost its passenger service on 10 September 1962. However, it was very busy with freight traffic, notably coal to Fiddlers Ferry power station. Due to repairs required to the large girder bridge (Latchford Bridge), which carried the line over the Manchester Ship Canal, and the availability of alternative routes, the line closed east of Latchford in July 1985. The 9F is passing a surviving LNWR signal by the signal box at Latchford with an empty coal train.

***Below* Wigan: 9F 2-10-0**

The 9F is heading north on the West Coast Main Line and is crossing the line from Wigan Wallgate to Southport via Burscough and Liverpool via Kirkby. The area where I took this photograph has since been redeveloped and is now an industrial estate.

Above Warrington Dallam Branch Sidings: 'Britannia' 4-6-2 No 70034 (formerly *Thomas Hardy*)

The feel of the industrial North West comes over in this picture of the 'Britannia' approaching Warrington in the winter of 1966/67 with an up parcels train, which includes a Royal Mail sorting coach. In the far distance the exhaust from another freight train can be seen approaching, which emphasises just how busy this line was in steam days. This 'Britannia' spent the last four years or so of its life on the London Midland Region.

Below Warrington: 'Britannia' 4-6-2

Taken at about the same time as the picture above, this unidentified 'Britannia' is climbing out of Warrington towards the girder bridge over the Manchester Ship Canal with a stopping train for Crewe, a typical duty during the last days of the class. In the foreground, protected by a lookout man, a permanent way worker is attending to a set of points.

Wigan: 5MT 4-6-0
Three workers probably coming off shift pause for a chat as the Class 5 heads south towards Warrington with a freight.

Wigan: 5MT 4-6-0

On this still winter afternoon the Class 5 is slowly heading north with a vans train. In the foreground a diesel multiple unit stands in the platform at Wigan Wallgate station.

Left Hoghton Bottoms: 5MT 4-6-0 No 45436
The stretch of line between Bamber Bridge and Blackburn ran through pleasant country, featuring quite steep gradients in the eastbound direction. Steam working on this line lasted until the very end. No 45436, which is passing over the viaduct over the River Darwen, almost made it to the end as well, but was withdrawn in April 1968.

Below Near Bamber Bridge: 8F 2-8-0
The stark outline of the trees sets off the 8F as is passes the attractive little level crossing on the 1 in 99 gradient with an eastbound train of coal empties.

Above **Near Rose Grove: 8F 2-8-0 No 48727**
Smartly turned-out No 48727 from Rose Grove shed looks fully in control of this westbound loaded coal train leaving its home town. The locomotive has lost its smokebox numberplate and has one painted on instead. It was one of the final batch of locomotives withdrawn by British Railways in August 1968.

Right **Between Hapton and Huncoat: 8F 2-8-0 No 48191**
Like sister locomotive No 48727, this 8F also survived at Rose Grove shed until the end. It is passing an upper-quadrant signal with another loaded train of power station coal.

Bamber Bridge: 8F 2-8-0 No 48167

The driver of Rose Grove shed's No 48167, working a train of eastbound coal empties, has opened up his locomotive in exhilarating style at the start of the 1 in 99/100 climb towards Blackburn. Surely this is a scene worthy of 'Steam's Last Stand'.

Hospital Crossing, Bamber Bridge: 8F 2-8-0s Nos 48308 and 48684

Hospital Crossing was located almost a mile east of Bamber Bridge station and is the setting for this eastbound loaded coal train. The M61 motorway now passes over the line roughly where No 48684 is.

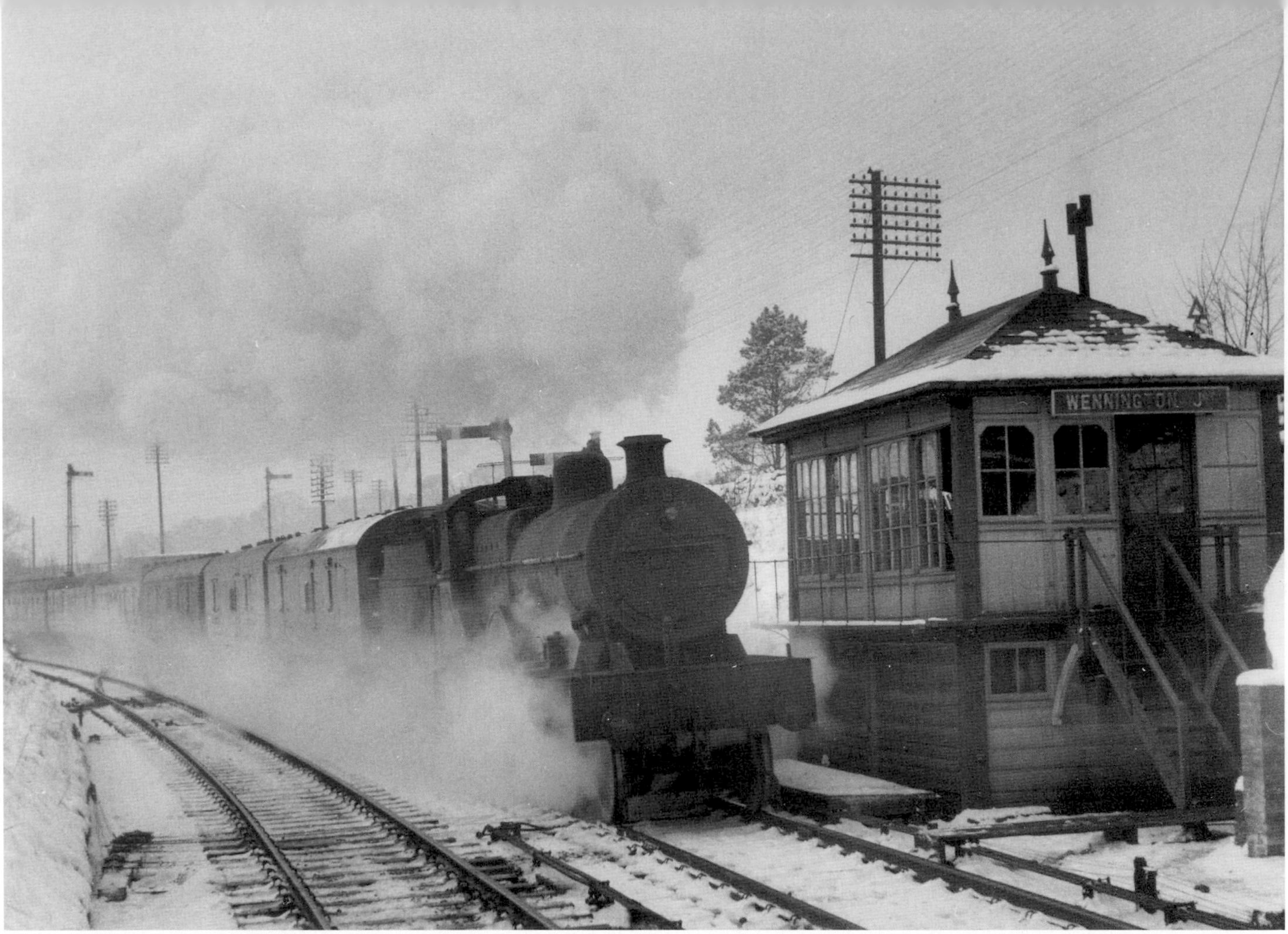
WENNINGTON J

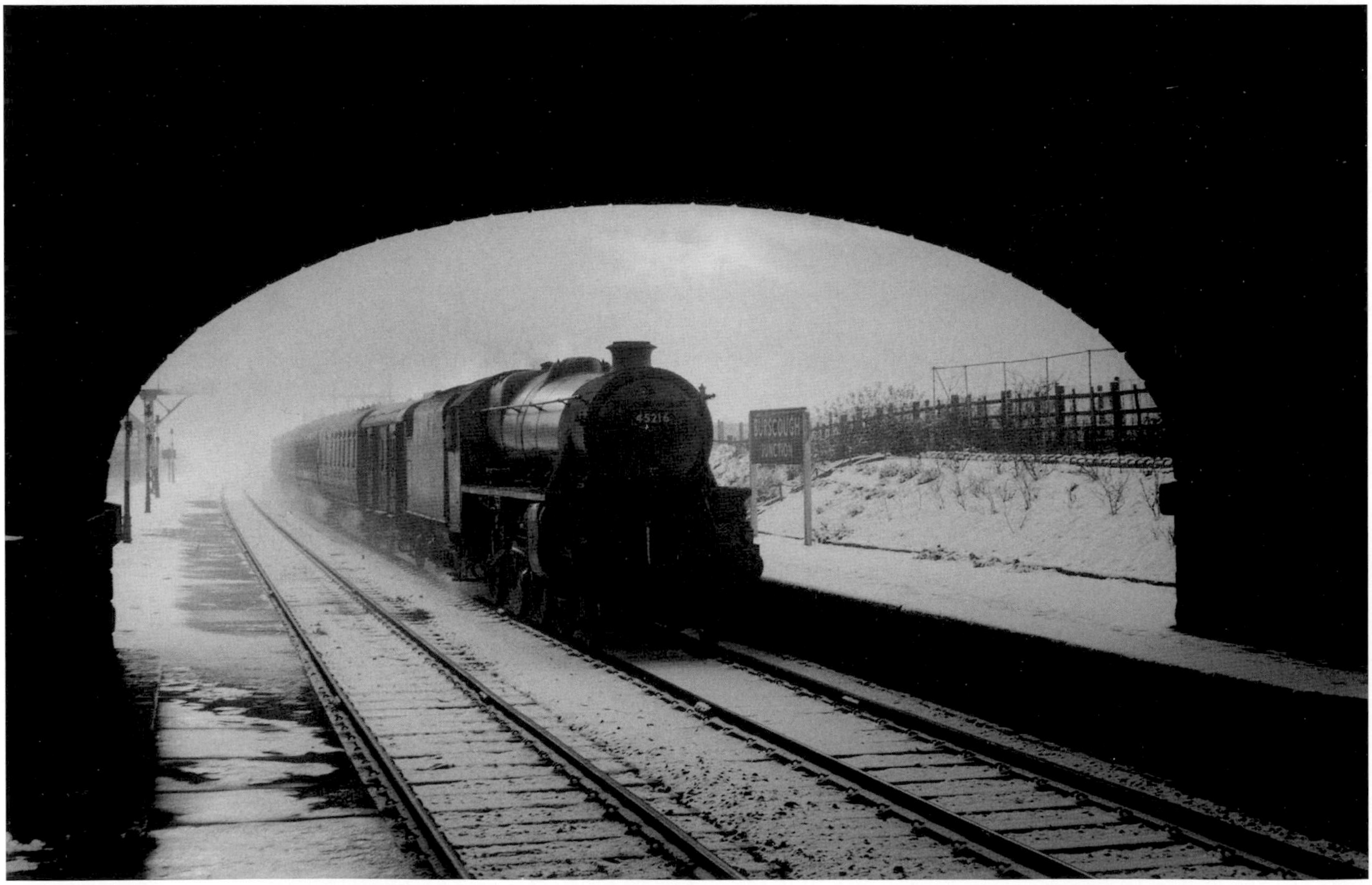
45216
BURSCOUGH
JUNCTION

Left **Wennington: 'Compound' 4-4-0**
Cold winters with snow and frost made steam photography in the North West particularly rewarding, as the next four pages show. Set off by the attractive Midland Railway signal box, one of Lancaster shed's old 'Compounds' is leaking badly as it struggles round the curve on the line from its home town with an eastbound train in early 1958.

Below left **Burscough Junction: 5MT 4-6-0 No 45216**
On this snowy but sunny morning the Class 5 is entering the station with a train from Liverpool Exchange to Preston. In early 1968 this line was one of the last to have steam rostered on fast passenger trains, which produced some lively running over this straight stretch of track. Driven by enthusiastic crews, Class 5s often attained speeds in the high 70s and low 80s in the Rufford and Maghull areas, on trains such as the 9.00am train from Liverpool Exchange and, in the opposite direction, the 9.25pm from Preston.

Right **Grayrigg: 'Britannia' 4-6-2 No 70001 Lord Hurcomb**
There has been a quite heavy fall of snow as No 70001 runs cautiously south down Grayrigg bank near Lambrigg with a freight. Judging by the pristine condition of the snow by the trackside, the permanent way men have not been about yet!

Below **Moore: Rebuilt 'Royal Scot' 4-6-0 No 46142 The York & Lancaster Regiment**
On this cold morning, with the frost still on the ground, the rebuilt 'Scot' has been reduced to freight haulage as it heads south. The locomotive was withdrawn in January 1964 from Carlisle (Upperby).

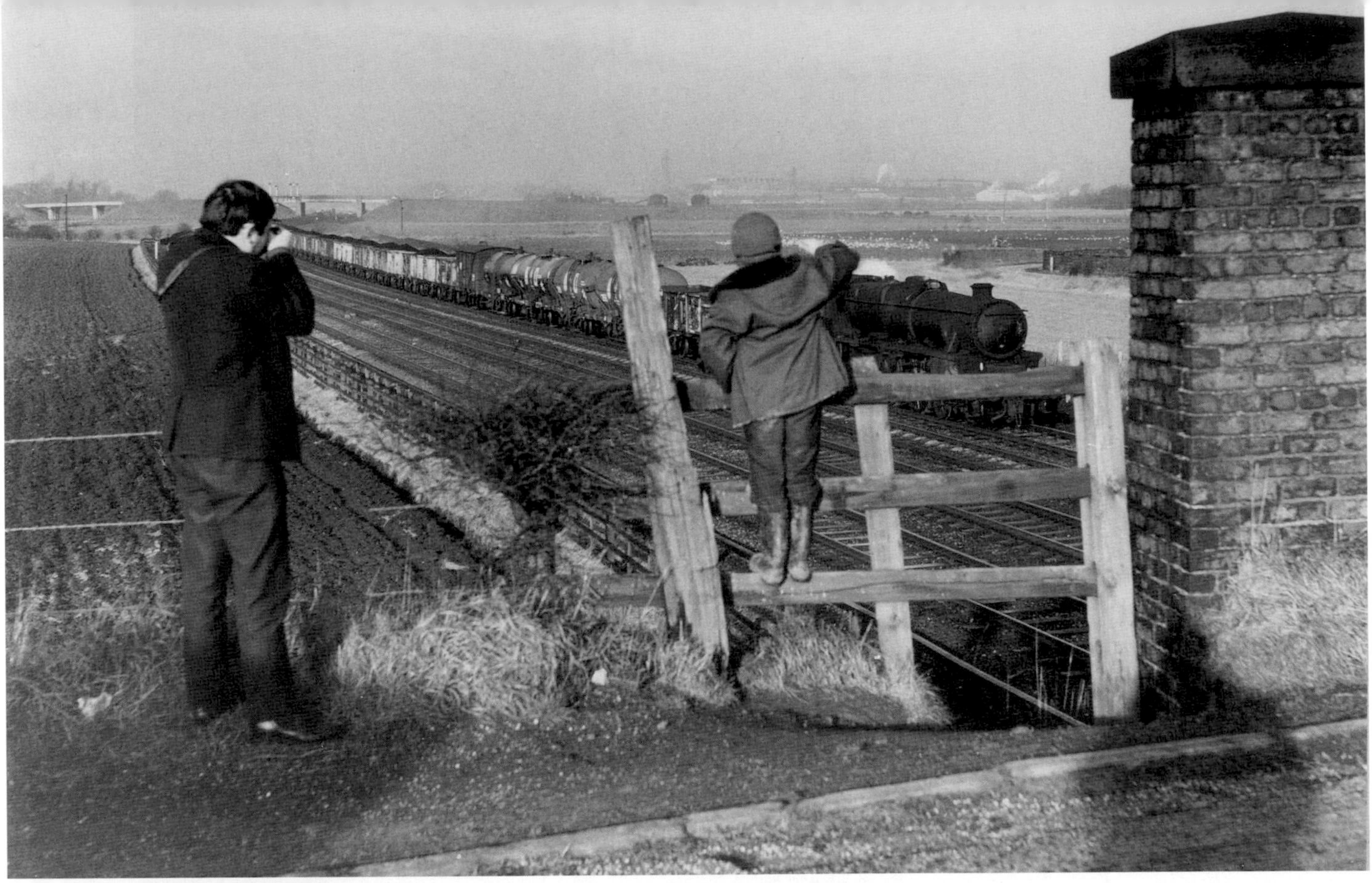

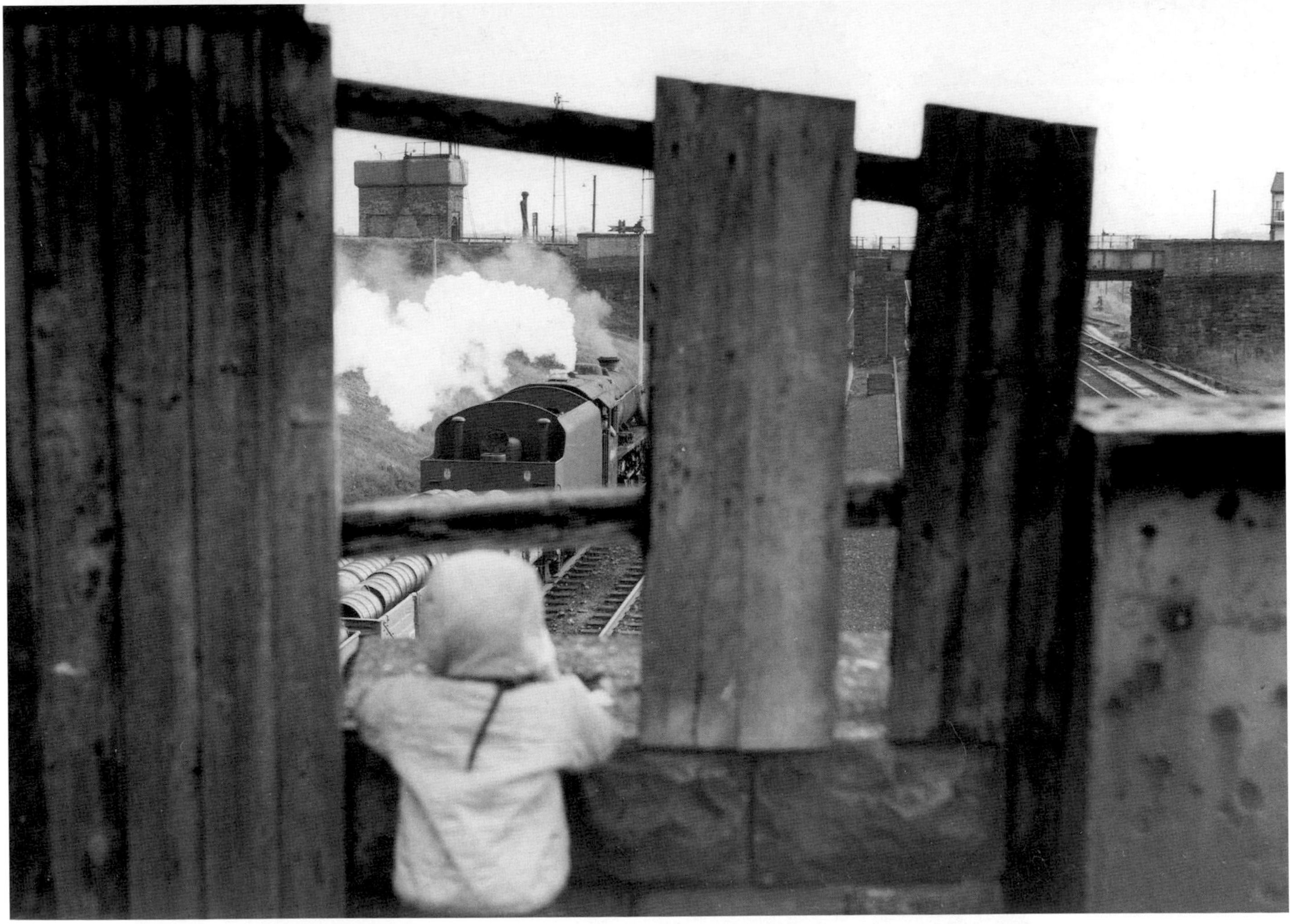

Left Winwick: 5MT 4-6-0
Two boys, part of the last generation of steam locospotters, enjoy the passing of an up freight, which consists mainly of power station coal.

Below left Near Springs Branch, Wigan: 5MT 4-6-0
Through a gap in a makeshift wooden fence, perhaps erected to stop young trainspotters leaning too far over the bridge parapet, my son watches a Class 5 going south near Wigan with an up freight.

Above Rose Grove shed
While I often had a permit, I have to admit that I 'bunked' many sheds in my youth, often guided to them by the street directions in Aidan L. Fuller's famous *British Locomotive Shed Directory*. How privileged these lads were, to be just in time to experience the magic of the working steam shed – perhaps it did not occur to them that they were to be the last in a long line of shed 'bunkers'. At the very end of steam, authority took a slightly more tolerant view of unauthorised visitors to the few remaining sheds, so these spotters did not perhaps have to fear a heart jolting shout of, 'Oi, you! Where d'you think you're going?' from a member of the shed staff!

Left Preston: 5MT 4-6-0 No 45342
As I mentioned on page 97, the Liverpool to Preston line was the setting for some fast running towards the end of steam. There was also the odd steam turn remaining on the line to Blackpool South, like the 8.50pm Saturdays-only train from Preston. No 45342 lasted until the very end of steam, and here it is at Preston surrounded by some admiring enthusiasts who avidly followed, or travelled on, these last passenger workings.

Newton Heath shed (9D): 5MT 4-6-0s
Here is the incomparable atmosphere of the working steam shed, which was soon to be lost for ever – light, shade and shafts of sunlight in the smoky air.

Right Rose Grove shed (10F)
Deep inside Rose Grove shed all is silent apart from the gentle hissing of steam from an 8F 2-8-0. The line of 'dead' locomotives on the left shows that steam working is almost at an end.

Below Edge Hill shed (8A)
I wished I had visited this shed when it was full of 7P and 8P locomotives in its heyday, but it was not to be. As it was, it hung on until 6 May 1968, not long after I took this picture of some of its remaining allocation of Class 5s and 8Fs. I do remember that the shed was quite difficult to find – as the *Shed Directory* said in an understated way, it was 'in a maze of lines east of Edge Hill station'. By 29 July 1968 there were only three locomotives left at the shed, all destined for scrapping.

Above **Rose Grove shed: 8F 2-8-0 No 48715**
I have taken this picture from rail level to capture the feeling of the end of steam. Spilt coal and clinker lie about the track, while to the left withdrawn locomotives are lined up by the side of the shed.

Above right **Newton Heath shed**
This was a task that was to become increasingly common at steam sheds in the North West, though rarely photographed. A fitter uses his oxy-acetylene equipment to remove the front numberplate from a Class 5 before it goes off for scrap. How many times his weekly wage would a Class 5 smokebox numberplate be worth these days, I wonder?

Right **Bolton shed**
Hundreds of locomotives were sold to private contractors at the end of steam, but a few were dismantled on-site, sometimes because they were unsafe to be moved. For example, *The Railway Observer* reported that 8F No 48469 was being cut up at the shed on 2 April 1968 as a fractured tyre made it unsafe to move. This dismembered corpse may well be the same 8F, though I was unable to record the locomotive's number to confirm its identity.

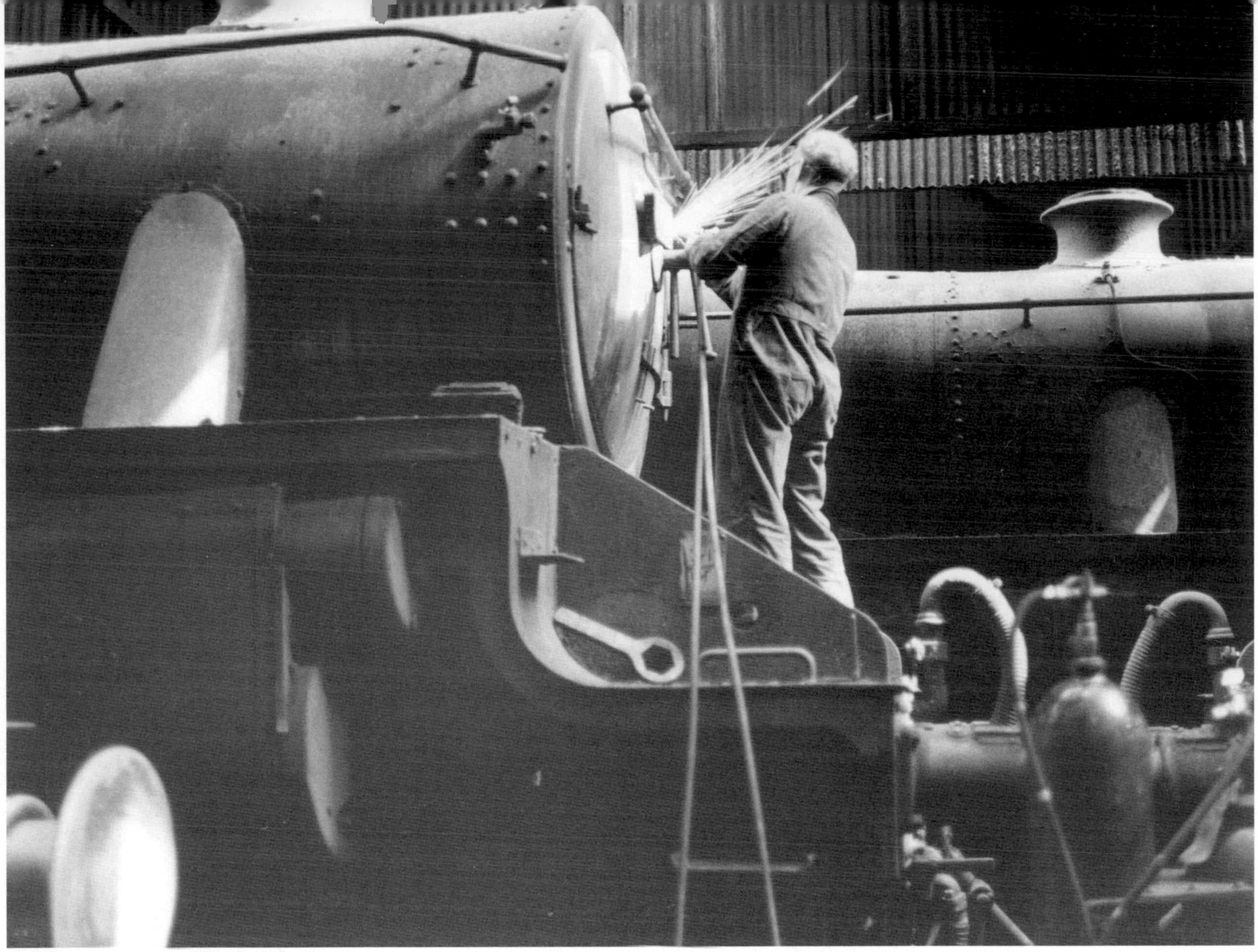

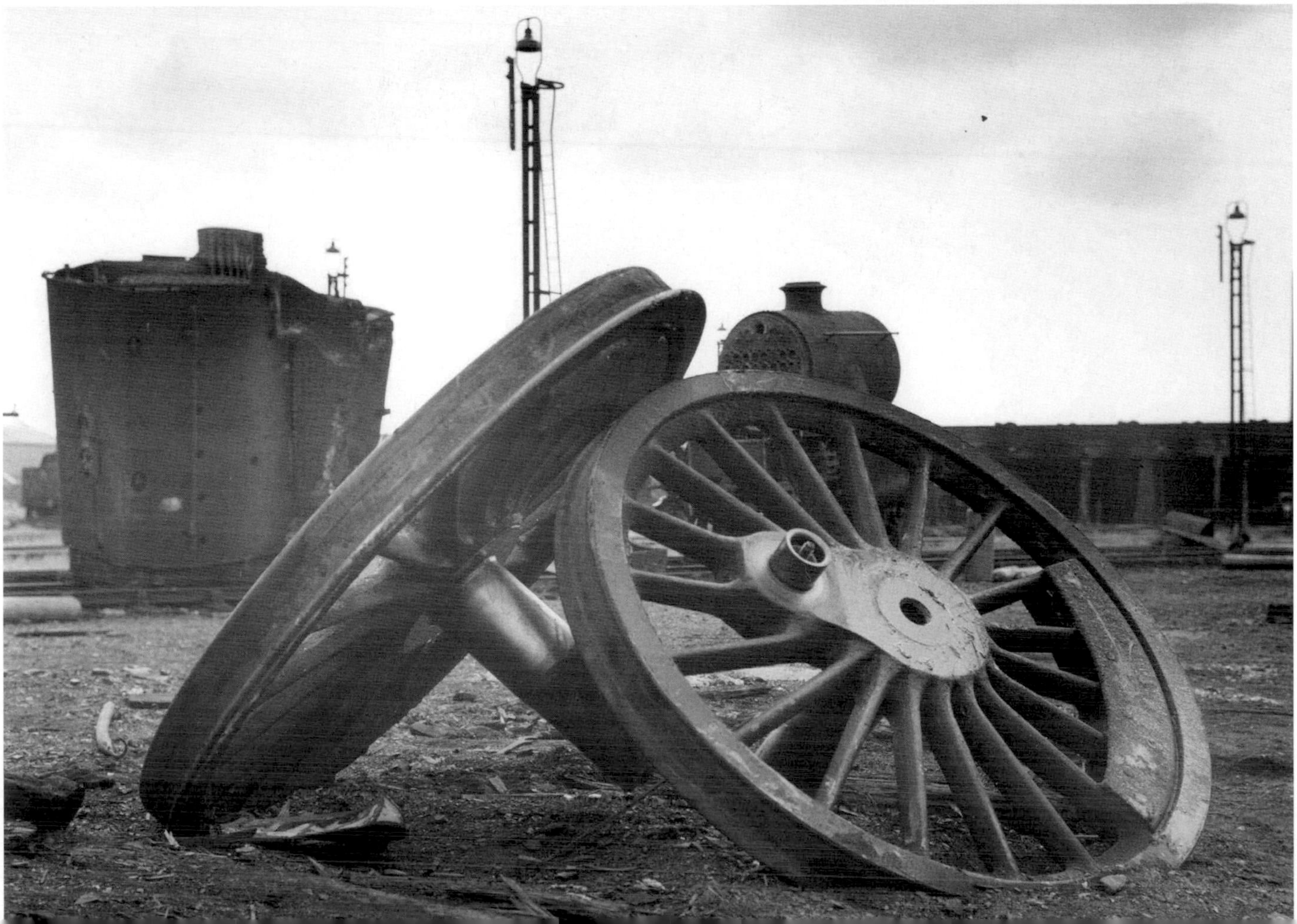

Lostock Hall shed: 8F 2-8-0 No 48476
Even at the end of steam it was possible to capture some pleasing images, not just
depressing lines of withdrawn locomotives. This puddle at Lostock Hall has given me
the chance to photograph this locomotive reflected in the water. A member of the shed
staff walking by the front of the 8F completes the picture. No 48476 piloted Standard
Class 5 No 73069 on the Railway Correspondence & Travel Society's rail tour on 4
August 1968.

Right **Lostock Hall shed: 5MT 4-6-0 and 8F 2-8-0**
In stark contrast to the last photograph, these two
locomotives have undertaken their final workings and
have been dumped on the 'withdrawn road' at the shed
ready to be taken away for scrap.

Below **Bolton shed: 5MT 4-6-0 and 8F 2-8-0**
'The quick and the dead' – contrasts at Bolton shed.
Working a coal train, an 8F passes by the scrap road at
Bolton shed where a Class 5 has had its motion
dismantled ready to be towed away.

Rose Grove shed: 8F 2-8-0s Nos 48666 and 48773
On 2 August 1968 No 48666 distinguished itself by being perhaps the last British Railways locomotive in service to be derailed. No 48773 was on hand to re-rail its recalcitrant sister locomotive as these two pages show. My son has taken advantage of the opportunity to get into the cab of the derailed 8F.

The second picture shows the derailed locomotive with No 48773 behind. This 8F was happily saved from scrap and is now based at the Severn Valley Railway.

No 48773 was then prepared to pull No 48666 back on to the rails. Note that the 8F sports a star by the cab-side number, which indicates that the coupled wheels have been specially balanced for higher speed running.

A little later No 48773 gives No 48666 a mighty heave, watched by a fascinated gallery of onlookers enjoying this unexpected 'end of steam' spectacle. After it was re-railed, which speaks volumes for the skill of the shed staff, the locomotive was placed on the 'withdrawn' road, its brief moment of celebrity over.

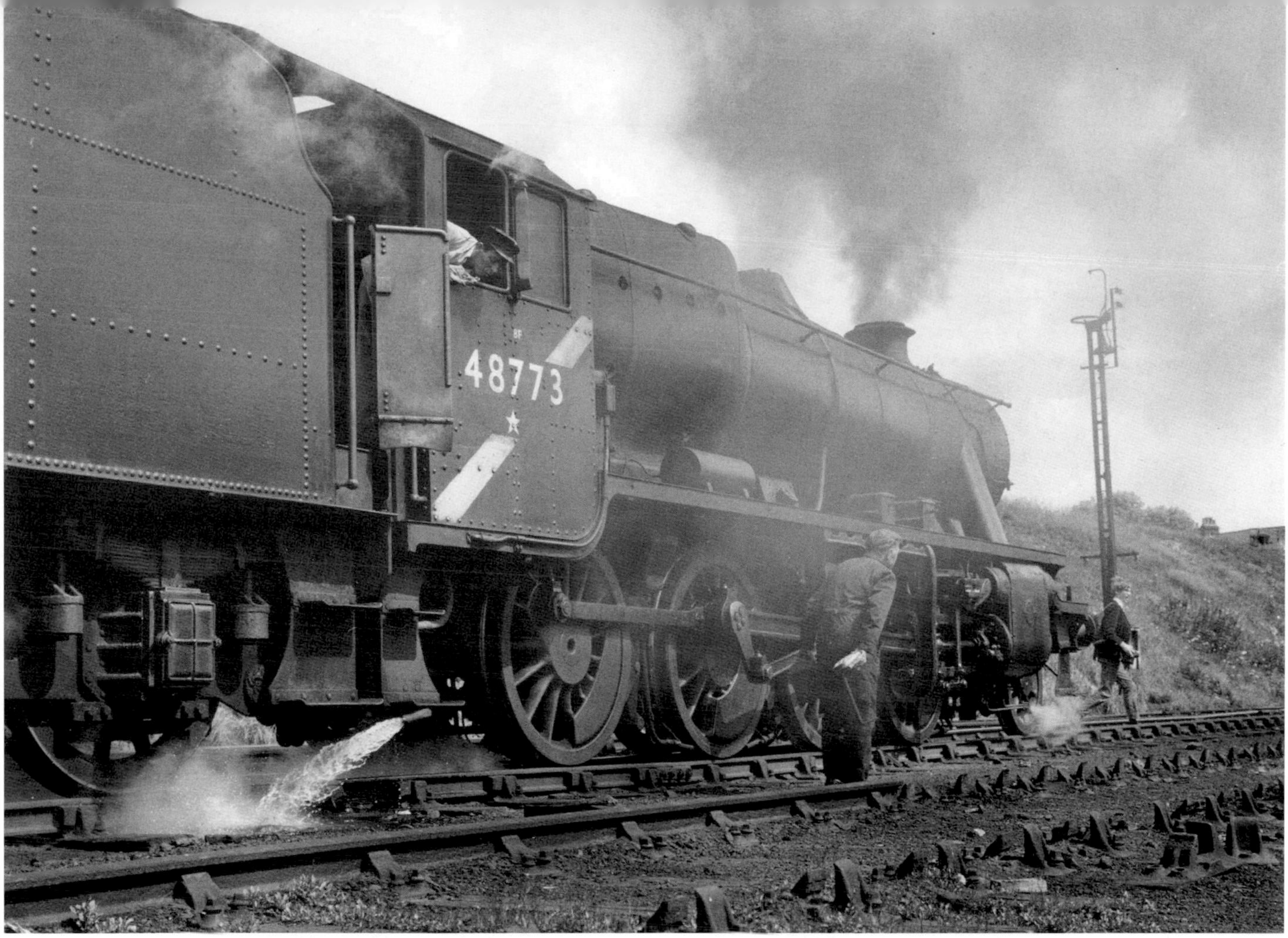
48773

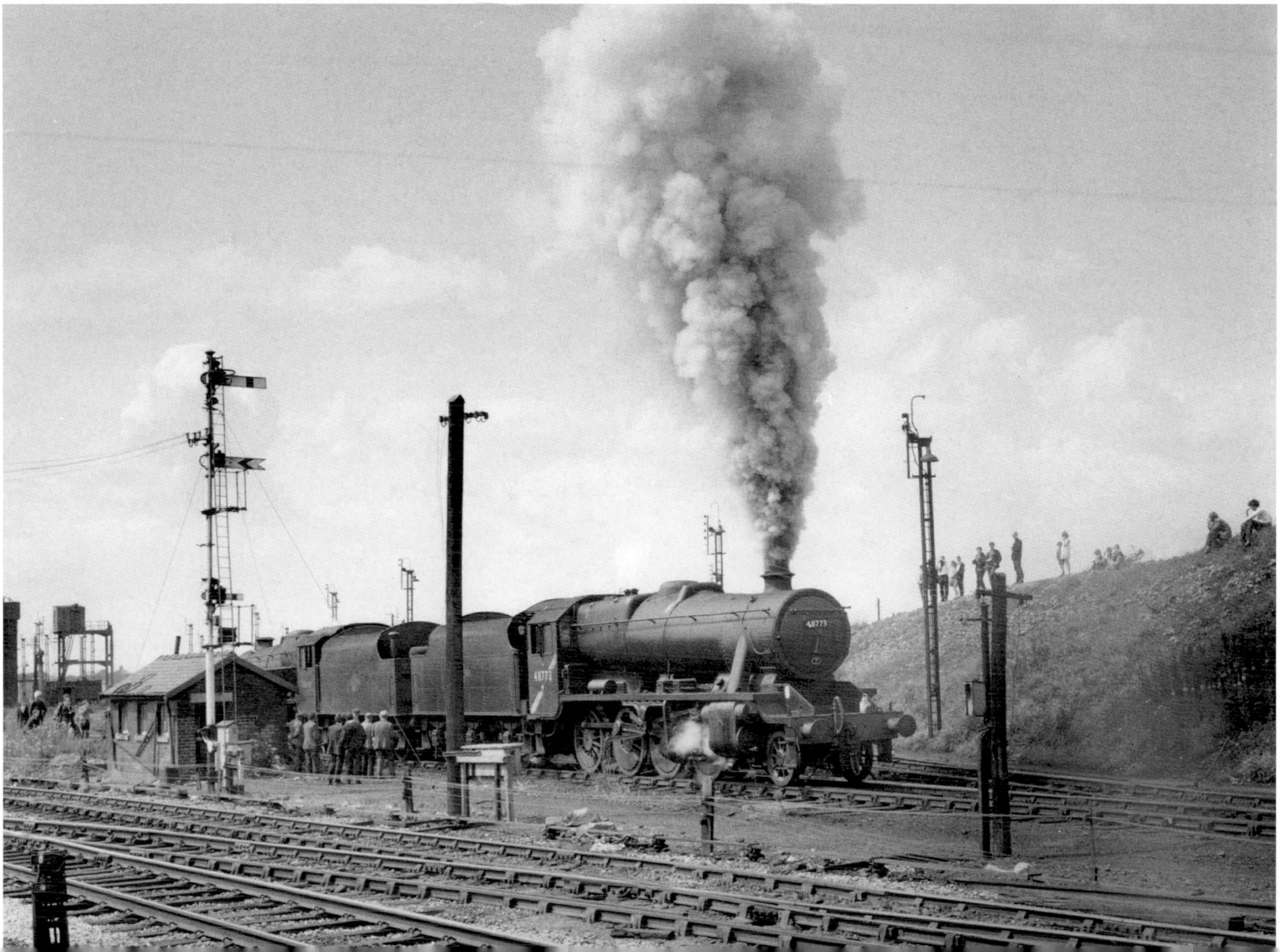

Left **Manchester Victoria: 5MT 4-6-0 No 45342**
Above **Preston: 5MT 4-6-0 No 45025**

Amongst the last steam main-line passenger workings was the 'Belfast Boat Express' between Manchester Victoria and Heysham. Its last runs were on 4 and 5 May 1968. Beautifully cleaned, No 45342 from Carnforth shed, complete with headboards (possibly courtesy of the renowned 'MNA', the Master Neverers Association), is ready to depart from Manchester Victoria. Watched by a large crowd of enthusiasts, it left at 8.55pm with a rake of blue and grey coaches.

The next morning the final return working was in the charge of Carnforth's popular No 45025, which is seen just south of Preston.

Right **Lostock Hall shed: 'Britannia' 4-6-2 No 70013** *Oliver Cromwell* **and Type 4 No D232** *Empress of Canada*

'The Rivals' – when the remaining 'Britannias' were withdrawn from Carlisle (Kingmoor) at the end of 1967, No 70013 was retained for use on special duties including the end-of-steam workings and as such was kept in smart condition. This picture was taken at the same time as that on the first page of this book. One of the English Electric 2,000hp Type 4 (later Class 40) diesels is seen in the foreground. These locomotives formed the first generation of diesels that progressively replaced steam on the principal main-line duties in the North West.

Near Darwen: 5MT 4-6-0s Nos 44874 and 45017
We have reached the very last day of steam working on British Railways, 4 August 1968, when a number of special trains were run to mark this sad occasion. Here is 1Z79, one of the Stephenson Locomotive Society specials from Manchester, heading south near Darwen.

Near Sough Tunnel: 5MT 4-6-0 No 45156 *Ayrshire Yeomanry*
No 45156 has to cope by itself with the eight coaches of the Bahamas Locomotive Society special 1T80 on the stiff climb to Sough Tunnel watched by a good crowd of photographers and well-wishers. Prominent on the embankment behind the locomotive are beds of rosebay willowherb, a prolific plant that blooms in July and August. I will always associate it with the end of steam, especially as the purple-red colour of its flowers almost seemed to mirror the maroon colour scheme of the London Midland Region at the time.

Above Darwen: 'Britannia' 4-6-2 No 70013 *Oliver Cromwell* and 5MT 4-6-0
No 44781
Below Entwistle: 5MT 4-6-0s Nos 44871 and 44894

Carrying a wreath on the front of its smokebox, No 70013, piloting No 44781, comes round the curve at Hollins Sidings, north of Darwen station, with 1Z74, a Locomotive Club of Great Britain tour that had originated in London.

At Entwistle, with its distinctive signal box perched above the tracks, 1Z78, a Stephenson Locomotive Society tour, coasts through the station hauled by the two smartly turned-out Class 5s. Given that this was the last day of steam working on British Railways, how low-key everything looks, compared with the crowds of photographers that often follow special steam trains today.

Hoghton: 5MT 4-6-0s Nos 45390 and 45025, and 5MT 4-6-0 No 45407 with Standard 5MT 4-6-0 No 73069

As dusk approached on 4 August I decided to go to the overbridge at Long Barn near Hoghton on the line out of Blackburn to see the last two specials pass. Both were running late but the light, though fading, was good enough for me to take the LCGB train as it sped by, No 45025 giving a blast on its hooter. A little later and running some 4 hours late there was only just about enough light left for me to photograph the RCTS special pass. *The Railway Observer* records that '…it was a thrilling climax to tear through Hoghton at 60mph with whistles sounding and spectators waving. All our passengers must have imprinted on their minds this final run down to Lostock Hall.' This train was a significant end for me, too, for it was my last photograph of steam on British Railways. As I went home through the gathering darkness, it was hard to realise that when the sun rose again the next day a strange silence would have descended on the railways of the North West – working steam had made its last stand.

INDEX